· A BOOK OF ·
CHRISTMAS
CAROLS

IN MEMORY OF
ELIZABETH POSTON

· A BOOK OF ·
CHRISTMAS
CAROLS

EDITED BY

ELIZABETH POSTON AND MALCOLM WILLIAMSON

ILLUMINATED BY

JANE LYDBURY

PRENTICE HALL PRESS
NEW YORK · LONDON · TORONTO · SYDNEY · TOKYO

PRENTICE HALL PRESS
GULF+WESTERN BUILDING
ONE GULF+WESTERN PLAZA
NEW YORK, NY 10023

LIBRARY OF CONGRESS CATALOGING-IN-PUBLICATION DATA
A BOOK OF CHRISTMAS CAROLS.
FOR VOICES AND PIANO.
 1. CAROLS, ENGLISH. 2. CHRISTMAS MUSIC. I. POSTON,
ELIZABETH, 1905-1987. II. WILLIAMSON, MALCOLM.
M2065.B7 1988   87-754819
 ISBN 0-13-079831-2

DESIGNED AND PRODUCED BY SHELDRAKE PRESS LTD
MUSIC TYPESETTING BY MUSICPAGE, SANDON, HERTFORDSHIRE
TYPESETTING BY GET SET, ROYSTON, HERTFORDSHIRE
COLOR ORIGINATION BY IMAGO PUBLISHING
PRINTED AND BOUND IN ITALY BY MONDADORI

10 9 8 7 6 5 4 3 2 1

FIRST PRENTICE HALL PRESS EDITION

SHELDRAKE PRESS LTD
188 CAVENDISH ROAD
LONDON SW12 0DA

EDITOR: SIMON RIGGE
DEPUTY EDITOR: DIANA DUBENS
ASSISTANT EDITOR: BARRIE CARSON TURNER
ART DIRECTION AND BOOK DESIGN: IVOR CLAYDON, BOB HOOK
EDITORIAL ASSISTANTS: JOAN LEE, HELEN RIDGE
PRODUCTION MANAGER: HUGH ALLAN
PRODUCTION ASSISTANT: HELEN SECCOMBE

ACKNOWLEDGEMENTS

Acknowledgements are made for permission to use copyright material granted by the following copyright owners: the Archive of Folk Culture, the Library of Congress, Washington D.C. for *The Cherry Tree Carol* (*Joseph and Mary*); Simon Campion, Campion Press for *Jesus Christ The Apple Tree*; Stainer & Bell Ltd for *On Christmas Night* and *Down in Yon Forest*, words and music collected by Ralph Vaughan Williams.

CONTENTS

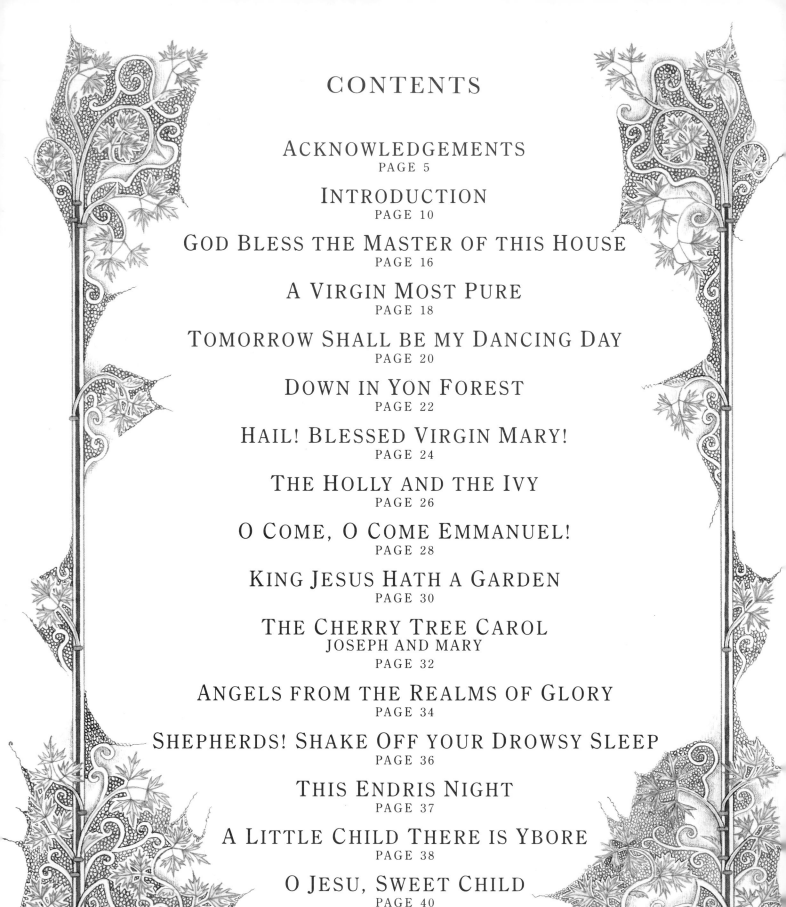

INTRODUCTION

The carol was already an old form of dance and song long before the birth of Christianity. This is worth remembering if only to counteract the popular idea that the carol emerged as a jolly sort of hymn in the Middle Ages and persisted into Dickensian times, surviving today as a cosy and highly commercial reminder of the comforts of the Victorian hearth. Even some dependable dictionaries give no source for the word 'carol' earlier than medieval French or English. But to find the true origins of the carol we have to look much further back into history and in doing so we find that a carol is not by any means the same thing as a hymn, and it is by no means exclusively wedded to Christmas, or even to the high feasts of Christianity.

Of their very nature hymns and psalms were dedicated by the human spirit, with due reverence, to one or more superior beings. In ancient Egypt, in the lands of the Bible, Greece and elsewhere, devotional dance, song and instrumental music were offered to a Deity or deities. Plato, Socrates' greatest disciple, commended the singing of hymns in the fifth and fourth centuries B.C. Carols on the other hand did not originally have a religious intention.

By Plato's time the universal popularity of the theatre as entertainment was long established. There was a chorus, acting, dancing and singing, frequently in alternation with the classical Greek flute-like instrument the *aulos*. The Greek word *choros* properly means a circling dance, as well as the chorus or choir that performed such dances. The compounded word *chor-aulos*, forerunner of the carol, can thus be said to have signified an often pleasurable form of entertainment. Plato was no killjoy, although such is sometimes claimed; but he sternly condemned pleasure for pleasure's sake, and that condemnation included all aspects of the theatre and of poetry, not to mention music, that were not aimed at truth and high seriousness. The fact that contemporary dramatists satirized Socrates simply made matters worse in Plato's eyes. So while hymns were encouraged, carols were less than admirable. To sing, play and dance for the deity was one thing; David did so before the Ark of the Covenant. To sing, play and dance for community earthly pleasure, quite another.

The ethical and moral distinctions between hymn and carol are highlighted in various periods of history. At times dancing was suppressed, and secular singing was approved while sacred singing was condemned. Authorities at other times applauded dancing in the secular world but not the sacred, or *vice versa*. All through history there have been those who would sing battle-hymns to a deity for victory, and more recently dance and sing political campaigning songs without a blink, but would never be caught dancing and singing devotional carols.

Of course, the religious controversies of the past are to most of us just past history, but we might usefully remind ourselves that still today hymns are of their nature religious poems and songs dedicated to God or to gods and goddesses, while carols are community expressions of celebration whether they be narrative or nonsense, symbolist or satirical.

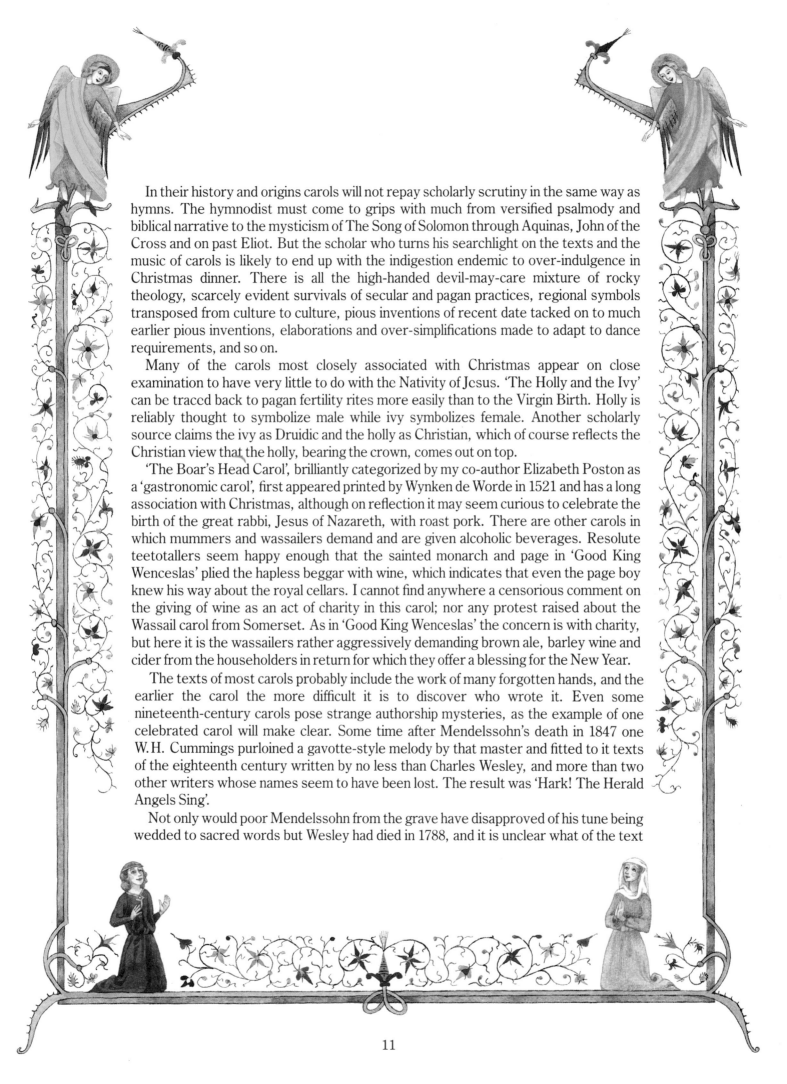

In their history and origins carols will not repay scholarly scrutiny in the same way as hymns. The hymnodist must come to grips with much from versified psalmody and biblical narrative to the mysticism of The Song of Solomon through Aquinas, John of the Cross and on past Eliot. But the scholar who turns his searchlight on the texts and the music of carols is likely to end up with the indigestion endemic to over-indulgence in Christmas dinner. There is all the high-handed devil-may-care mixture of rocky theology, scarcely evident survivals of secular and pagan practices, regional symbols transposed from culture to culture, pious inventions of recent date tacked on to much earlier pious inventions, elaborations and over-simplifications made to adapt to dance requirements, and so on.

Many of the carols most closely associated with Christmas appear on close examination to have very little to do with the Nativity of Jesus. 'The Holly and the Ivy' can be traced back to pagan fertility rites more easily than to the Virgin Birth. Holly is reliably thought to symbolize male while ivy symbolizes female. Another scholarly source claims the ivy as Druidic and the holly as Christian, which of course reflects the Christian view that the holly, bearing the crown, comes out on top.

'The Boar's Head Carol', brilliantly categorized by my co-author Elizabeth Poston as a 'gastronomic carol', first appeared printed by Wynken de Worde in 1521 and has a long association with Christmas, although on reflection it may seem curious to celebrate the birth of the great rabbi, Jesus of Nazareth, with roast pork. There are other carols in which mummers and wassailers demand and are given alcoholic beverages. Resolute teetotallers seem happy enough that the sainted monarch and page in 'Good King Wenceslas' plied the hapless beggar with wine, which indicates that even the page boy knew his way about the royal cellars. I cannot find anywhere a censorious comment on the giving of wine as an act of charity in this carol; nor any protest raised about the Wassail carol from Somerset. As in 'Good King Wenceslas' the concern is with charity, but here it is the wassailers rather aggressively demanding brown ale, barley wine and cider from the householders in return for which they offer a blessing for the New Year.

The texts of most carols probably include the work of many forgotten hands, and the earlier the carol the more difficult it is to discover who wrote it. Even some nineteenth-century carols pose strange authorship mysteries, as the example of one celebrated carol will make clear. Some time after Mendelssohn's death in 1847 one W.H. Cummings purloined a gavotte-style melody by that master and fitted to it texts of the eighteenth century written by no less than Charles Wesley, and more than two other writers whose names seem to have been lost. The result was 'Hark! The Herald Angels Sing'.

Not only would poor Mendelssohn from the grave have disapproved of his tune being wedded to sacred words but Wesley had died in 1788, and it is unclear what of the text (culled from his 6,500 hymn texts) is actually his. In addition Mendelssohn (1809-1847) was charged with deliberately stealing the tune from Dr Pepusch (1667-1752) in whose opera of 1715, *Venus and Adonis*, it appeared as the 'Song of Mars'. Pepusch is remembered mainly for the writing of an overture and for orchestrating 69 folk melodies for John Gay's *Beggar's Opera* in 1728; further, the end of his life found him in London a luminary of the Academy of Antient Musick, all of which indicates that the 'Song of Mars' may not have been original even to him. Mendelssohn is charitably, and I think correctly, cleared by Elizabeth Poston of the charge of deliberate theft. As for Pepusch and Cummings and all the others who had a hand in this project, it certainly seems easier to render unto God the things that are God's than to render authorship unto the correct Caesar. One definite thing about 'Hark! The Herald Angels Sing' is that in 1856, out of a nest of geniuses and kleptomaniacs, there was born a standardized version which shows no signs of being dislodged from the popular eminence it enjoys.

Even if authorship can be established, the author's reasoning and good scholarship may not. The usually admirable collector of carols J.M. Neale (1818-1866) took the tunes of two secular spring carols and created enduring texts for them which are entirely without historical or even mythical antecedents, and are not even seasonally related to their original Latin words. One of these carols is 'Good King Wenceslas'. Neale had shamelessly invented a pious legend about an authentic sainted king, rather like a doctor telling cheery fibs to a dying patient on the premise that, true or not, it uplifts the spirits. If Elizabeth Poston, Percy Dearmer and other scholars had their way, the beautiful tune of 'Good King Wenceslas' would be restored to its rightful form as a dancing spring carol, and out into the deep, crisp and even snow, the cruel frost and rude wind would go Neale's pious text. But this seems unlikely to happen.

I think that no admiration is adequate for Elizabeth Poston's piercing researches into, and approval of, the carols we know and ought to know today. Where she launches out with blistering condemnation, she cites verifiable reasons for her views. Nonetheless in her collections she is prepared to sanction carols whose popularity outweighs their extrinsic value; and has a fine common-sense go at legitimizing artistic and historic bastardy where it is practical.

Until the night before her death Elizabeth Poston was working on the present volume. Although I should have loved to work with her on it, she needed no collaborator except a continuance of life, and that was denied her. She left this world peacefully on 18th March 1987 at the age of 81. I mourn her death, firstly because she was a friend that I and others loved, secondly because she was a great composer, thirdly because she was also a scholar of great depth which was tempered by common sense.

In our proximity in her last years, it was my privilege to study and absorb some of Elizabeth Poston's thinking on the carol. Elizabeth had worked with such great composers and compilers of carols, hymns and folksongs as Ralph Vaughan Williams, while at the same time she was merciless with her tongue to those that she felt had commercialized the carol without due respect for authenticity and historicism. She knew what to touch and adapt; she knew what to leave alone, and living later than Vaughan Williams and his contemporaries Elizabeth both benefitted by their expertise and was able to travel more freely across the world, guided by infallible instinct as to what to seek and where. To her we owe the dissemination of carols from the North American heartland and from unimagined corners of Europe, as well as authentication of many old carols, not to mention the debunking of some pious frauds cherished by the nineteenth century and since.

Except for one carol, 'Brightest and Best of the Sons of the Morning', the selection in this book is Elizabeth's; and in my view a jewel in the selection is her own original 'Jesus Christ the Apple Tree', which gains ground every year in the canon of carols popularly sung. Indeed, the world being what it is, it may be a matter of time only before the attribution 'Trad. arr. E. Poston' is mistakenly placed above the music.

The text, an extraordinary *trouvaille*, is by an unknown poet, and was plucked by Elizabeth from a collection *Divine Hymns and Spiritual Songs* compiled by one Joshua Smith, and issued in New Hampshire in 1784. Perhaps it is more than just chance that Elizabeth chose this surrealist text, almost an anachronism in eighteenth-century North America and probably based on earlier sources. Concluding her introduction to *The Second Penguin Book of Christmas Carols* which she edited after Vaughan Williams' death, drawing largely on North American carols, she writes: 'The recurrent imagery of the Tree of Life has many forms. Mother Ann Lee, Shaker foundress and mystic, had a vision of America: "I saw a large tree, every leaf of which shone with such brightness as made it appear like a torch."' While these lines end a general commentary on Christmas Song and Dance in black America, Mother Ann's words seem to have inspired the choice of verse and the composition of the music.

Melodically and harmonically, 'Jesus Christ the Apple Tree' is all on white notes (thinking in keyboard terms) but its musical procedures defy analysis in any traditional way. While it is perpetually unpredictable, since it functions neither tonally nor modally, and obeys no conventional laws of part-writing, it stretches forward into its own future, and yet it seems, as in medieval music, to have C as its tonic and G as its final. Simple to perform, yet radiantly rich, after one has performed it a few times the unpredictability vanishes and one says, 'But of course! It had to be like that!' – a not uncommon reaction to great music.

The persistent tale of Elizabeth's having composed 'Jesus Christ the Apple Tree' in a garage while waiting for her car to be repaired exists in as many versions as a popular carol, and while Elizabeth would undoubtedly have corroborated every version of the tale, it is no more likely to be founded in fact than Neale's words for 'Good King Wenceslas'.

Around the age of 80, Elizabeth Poston fought one-woman battles with the telephone system authorities and with the municipal authorities who closed down her road in Hertfordshire for repairs. In both cases she astonished everybody by emerging victorious. And so it was with her scholarship. She pursued and reached the heart of the matter, which in the case of the carol meant many a trek into historical and geographical darknesses, never losing sight of the essential dance facet or the human ecstasy that cause a carol to be different from a hymn.

It was Elizabeth's copious knowledge of the dance of the past, as executed both by gentles and simples, and of early instruments and their uses, many now obsolete, that informed such works as *Welcome, Child of Mary*, a major achievement where she brings an authenticity that defies criticism while speaking to our own time.

It would have been an impertinence for me to open discussion on religious affiliation in a sectarian sense with Elizabeth. Faith of her own private kind shines through her work and in her writings. In her collections of carols she moves effortlessly across the broad spectrum from Jewish to Catholic, Anglican and so-called Non-Conformist worlds to the seemingly distant fringes of isolated Moravian and even more isolated sects of the American Deep South. It is clear, although there is but one exclusively Jewish carol (if I may be forgiven for calling it a carol, a word that through the tragedies of history is not acceptable any longer in the synagogue), that this volume in its sacred

and secular aspects bestrides the chasms of sectarian division, as Elizabeth Poston more than once in print advocated as desirable. She also carried her beliefs into practice. I was deputed by her to bring from the Soviet Union in 1987 all the folk songs representing all the Soviet republics that I could find. The project that she planned after this volume was to have been an accessible, simple collection of folk music from the Soviet Union.

The author of countless articles, Elizabeth wrote none on the subject of faith; but, unlike her lifelong friend E.M. Forster (who had once lived in the house where Elizabeth spent most of her life, immortalized as Howard's End), and wrote 'I do not believe in Belief', she believed, although she was sage enough not to want to raid the spiritually inarticulate. She believed in the Human Family.

On the night before she died, Elizabeth Poston had worked on a North of England version of the Wassail carol, which bears close resemblance to the commonly sung Somerset text. There is in both a request for bread and cheese as well as for domestically brewed liquor. The manuscript of Elizabeth's, left for the ink to dry, was found untouched along with her source materials on her desk after her death. It seems appropriate that her last earthly labour was devoted to arranging a carol of untraceable ancestry which is redolent of charity, hospitality, the good life, and to the mingling of rich and poor in the Human Family; as similarly within days of her death a vast choir with harp accompaniment sang the first performance of her *A Settled Rest* at the Royal Albert Hall, her last original, but folksong-based, composition.

How she would have enjoyed the opening announcements that evening. Among the introductory remarks from the platform, which included the reading of a Royal telegram of greeting and messages from well-wishers, there was a small catalogue of regrets from people who had been overtaken by some or other catastrophe. Friends of Elizabeth knew that she would have enjoyed (and I quote only from memory) the Mark Twainish announcement: 'Miss Elizabeth Poston cannot be with us tonight as she died earlier this week.'

Elizabeth left the list of carols for this volume in alphabetical order. It was not her intention that they should be published in that order, nor with any regard to the putative order of composition chronologically. Since most carols nowadays have acquired a strong religious connotation and are intended to celebrate the Nativity of Christ it seemed sensible to be guided by biblical chronology, and to arrange them to cover the foretelling of the birth of Jesus, the archangel's Annunciation, the night that we now call Christmas Eve when the star appeared and the Holy Child was born, Christmas Day, the feast day of Stephen the Martyr (Boxing Day) and the feast of the Epiphany (prudently placed by the Church well after the Nativity, and in many countries the most important day of celebration with the giving of presents). This ordering cannot be precisely kept, since some carol texts stretch from the prophecies of the Old Testament, through the Nativity, past the Epiphany, and on to a few lines of ethical and moral instruction of the type taught in a latter-day Sunday school:

Christian children all must be
Mild, obedient, good as he.

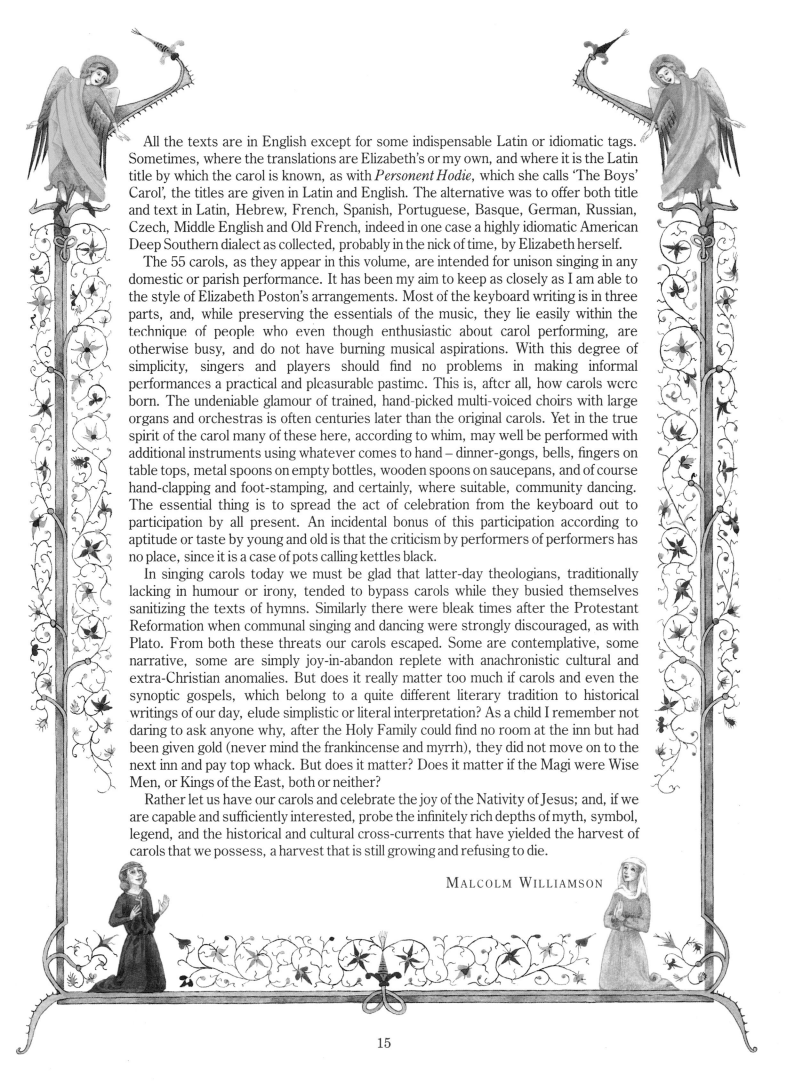

All the texts are in English except for some indispensable Latin or idiomatic tags. Sometimes, where the translations are Elizabeth's or my own, and where it is the Latin title by which the carol is known, as with *Personent Hodie*, which she calls 'The Boys' Carol', the titles are given in Latin and English. The alternative was to offer both title and text in Latin, Hebrew, French, Spanish, Portuguese, Basque, German, Russian, Czech, Middle English and Old French, indeed in one case a highly idiomatic American Deep Southern dialect as collected, probably in the nick of time, by Elizabeth herself.

The 55 carols, as they appear in this volume, are intended for unison singing in any domestic or parish performance. It has been my aim to keep as closely as I am able to the style of Elizabeth Poston's arrangements. Most of the keyboard writing is in three parts, and, while preserving the essentials of the music, they lie easily within the technique of people who even though enthusiastic about carol performing, are otherwise busy, and do not have burning musical aspirations. With this degree of simplicity, singers and players should find no problems in making informal performances a practical and pleasurable pastime. This is, after all, how carols were born. The undeniable glamour of trained, hand-picked multi-voiced choirs with large organs and orchestras is often centuries later than the original carols. Yet in the true spirit of the carol many of these here, according to whim, may well be performed with additional instruments using whatever comes to hand – dinner-gongs, bells, fingers on table tops, metal spoons on empty bottles, wooden spoons on saucepans, and of course hand-clapping and foot-stamping, and certainly, where suitable, community dancing. The essential thing is to spread the act of celebration from the keyboard out to participation by all present. An incidental bonus of this participation according to aptitude or taste by young and old is that the criticism by performers of performers has no place, since it is a case of pots calling kettles black.

In singing carols today we must be glad that latter-day theologians, traditionally lacking in humour or irony, tended to bypass carols while they busied themselves sanitizing the texts of hymns. Similarly there were bleak times after the Protestant Reformation when communal singing and dancing were strongly discouraged, as with Plato. From both these threats our carols escaped. Some are contemplative, some narrative, some are simply joy-in-abandon replete with anachronistic cultural and extra-Christian anomalies. But does it really matter too much if carols and even the synoptic gospels, which belong to a quite different literary tradition to historical writings of our day, elude simplistic or literal interpretation? As a child I remember not daring to ask anyone why, after the Holy Family could find no room at the inn but had been given gold (never mind the frankincense and myrrh), they did not move on to the next inn and pay top whack. But does it matter? Does it matter if the Magi were Wise Men, or Kings of the East, both or neither?

Rather let us have our carols and celebrate the joy of the Nativity of Jesus; and, if we are capable and sufficiently interested, probe the infinitely rich depths of myth, symbol, legend, and the historical and cultural cross-currents that have yielded the harvest of carols that we possess, a harvest that is still growing and refusing to die.

MALCOLM WILLIAMSON

GOD BLESS THE MASTER
OF THIS HOUSE

TRADITIONAL ENGLISH, FURRY DAY CAROL,
ARR. M.W.

God bless the __ mas - ter __ of this __ house, And __ all that are __ there - in - a, And to be - gin this __ Christ - mas - tide With __ mirth now let __ us __ sing - a! The Sa - viour of all ___ peo - - ple Up - - on this time __ was __ born - a, Who did from death de - - li - ver __ us, When __ we were left __ for - lorn - a.

GOD BLESS THE MASTER OF THIS HOUSE

1 God bless the master of this house,
  And all that are therein-a,
  And to begin this Christmastide
  With mirth now let us sing-a!

    The Saviour of all people
    Upon this time was born-a,
    Who did from death deliver us,
    When we were left forlorn-a.

2 Then let us all most merry be,
  And sing with cheerful voice-a,
  For we have good occasion now
  This time for to rejoice-a.

3 Then sing with voices cheerfully,
  For Christ this time was born-a,
  Who did from death deliver us
  When we were left forlorn-a.

Traditional English

VIRGIN MOST PURE

Flowing

TRADITIONAL ENGLISH, ARR. M.W.

A vir-gin most pure, as the pro-phets do tell, Hath brought forth a Baby, as it hath be-fell, To be our Re-dee-mer from death, hell and sin, Which A-dam's trans-gress-ion hath wrap-pèd us in:

Aye and there-fore be merry, re-joice and be you

1 A virgin most pure, as the prophets do tell,
  Hath brought forth a Baby, as it hath befell,
  To be our Redeemer from death, hell and sin,
  Which Adam's transgression hath wrappèd us in:

    Aye and therefore be merry, rejoice and be you merry,
    Set sorrows aside;
    Christ Jesus our Saviour was born on this tide.

2 At Bethlem in Jewry a city there was,
  Where Joseph and Mary together did pass,
  And there to be taxèd with many one mo',
  For Caesar commanded the same should be so:

3 But when they had entered the city so fair,
  A number of people so mighty was there,
  That Joseph and Mary, whose substance was small
  Could find in the inn there no lodging at all:

4 Then they were constrained in a stable to lie,
  Where oxen and asses they used for to tie;
  Their lodging so simple, they held it no scorn,
  But against the next morning our Saviour was born:

5 The King of all Glory to the world being brought,
  Small store of fine linen to wrap him was sought:
  And when she had swaddled her young Son so sweet,
  Within an ox-manger she laid him to sleep:

6 Then God sent an angel from heaven so high,
  To certain poor shepherds in fields where they lie,
  And bade them no longer in sorrow to stay,
  Because that our Saviour was born on this day.

7 Then presently after, the shepherds did spy
  A number of angels that stood in the sky,
  They joyfully talkèd, and sweetly did sing,
  To God be all glory, our heavenly King.

Traditional English

TOMORROW SHALL BE MY DANCING DAY

Lightly, in dance rhythm

TRADITIONAL ENGLISH, ARR. M.W.

To - mor-row shall be ___ my danc - ing day: I

would ___ my true ___ love did ___ so chance To ___

see the le - gend of ___ my play, To

call my true ___ love to ___ my dance:

20

TOMORROW SHALL BE MY DANCING DAY

Sing O my _ love, O _ my love, my love, my

love; This have I done _ for my _ true love.

1 Tomorrow shall be my dancing day:
    I would my true love did so chance
To see the legend of my play,
    To call my true love to my dance:

  Sing O my love, O my love, my love, my love;
     This have I done for my true love.

2 Then was I born of a virgin pure,
    Of her I took fleshly substance;
Thus was I knit to man's nature;
    To call my true love to my dance:

3 In a manger laid and wrapped I was,
    So very poor, this was my chance,
Betwixt an ox and a silly poor ass,
    To call my true love to my dance:

Traditional English from William Sandys, 1833

21

DOWN IN YON FOREST

Slowly, flexible and reflective

TRADITIONAL ENGLISH, ARR. E.P.

Down in yon fo-rest there stands__ a hall: *The bells__ of Pa-ra-dise*

I heard them ring: It's co-vered all o-ver with

pur-ple and pall: *And I love my Lord Je-sus a-bove a-ny-thing.*

DOWN IN YON FOREST

1 Down in yon forest there stands a hall:
   The bells of Paradise I heard them ring:
   It's covered all over with purple and pall:
   And I love my Lord Jesus above anything.

2 In that hall there stands a bed:
   It's covered all over with scarlet so red:

3 At the bed-side there lies a stone:
   Which the sweet Virgin Mary knelt upon:

4 Under that bed there runs a flood:
   The one half runs water, the other runs blood:

5 At the bed's foot there grows a thorn:
   Which ever blows blossom since he was born:

6 Over that bed the moon shines bright:
   Denoting our Saviour was born this night:

Traditional English
Tune and text collected by
Ralph Vaughan Williams, 1872-1958

HAIL! BLESSED VIRGIN MARY!

Rather slow and exultant

ITALIAN, 1689, ARR. M.W.

Hail! Bles - sed Vir - gin Ma - ry! For so, when

he did meet thee Spake migh - ty Ga - bri -

- el, - and thus we greet thee. Come

weal, come woe, our hymn shall ne - ver va - ry. ____

____ Hail! Bles - sed Vir - gin Ma - ry! Hail!

Bles - sed Vir - gin Ma - - ry!

HAIL! BLESSED VIRGIN MARY!

1 Hail! Blessed Virgin Mary!
   For so, when he did meet thee
   Spake mighty Gabriel,
       and thus we greet thee.
   Come weal, come woe, our
       hymn shall never vary.
   Hail! Blessed Virgin Mary!
   Hail! Blessed Virgin Mary!

2 Ave! Ave Maria!
   To gladden priest and people
   The angelus shall ring
       from every steeple,
   To sound his virgin birth.
       Alleluìa!
   Ave! Ave Maria!
   Ave! Ave Maria!

3 Archangels chant, 'Hosanna!'
   And, 'Holy! Holy! Holy!'
   Before the Infant born
       of thee, thou lowly,
   Aye – maiden child of
       Joachim and Anna.
   Archangels chant Hosanna!
   Archangels chant Hosanna!

George Ratcliffe Woodward, 1848-1934

THE HOLLY AND THE IVY

TRADITIONAL ENGLISH, COLLECTED BY
CECIL JAMES SHARP, 1859-1924, ARR. E.P.

Rather fast, light and flowing

The hol-ly and the i-vy, When they are both full grown, Of all the trees that are in the wood, The hol-ly bears the crown: The ris-ing of the sun And the run-ning of the deer, The play-ing of the mer-ry or-gan, Sweet sing-ing in the choir.

THE HOLLY AND
THE IVY

1 The holly and the ivy,
When they are both full grown,
Of all the trees that are in the wood,
The holly bears the crown:

The rising of the sun
And the running of the deer,
The playing of the merry organ,
Sweet singing in the choir.

2 The holly bears a blossom
As white as the lily flower,
And Mary bore sweet Jesus Christ
To be our sweet Saviour:

3 The holly bears a berry
As red as any blood,
And Mary bore sweet Jesus Christ
To do poor sinners good:

4 The holly bears a prickle
As sharp as any thorn,
And Mary bore sweet Jesus Christ
On Christmas day in the morn:

5 The holly bears a bark
As bitter as any gall,
And Mary bore sweet Jesus Christ
For to redeem us all:

6 The holly and the ivy,
When they are both full grown,
Of all the trees that are in the wood,
The holly bears the crown:

Traditional English

O COME, O COME EMMANUEL!

PLAINCHANT ADAPTED BY
THOMAS HELMORE, 1811-1890, ARR. M.W.

O come, O come, Em-man - - nu - el! And ran - som cap - tive Is - - ra - el, That mourns in lone - ly e - xile here Un - til the Son of God _____ ap - pear: Re - joice! Re - joice! Em - ma - - nu - el Shall come to thee, O Is - - ra - el.

O COME, O COME EMMANUEL!

Veni, veni, Emmanuel

1 O come, O come, Emmanuel!
   And ransom captive Israel,
   That mourns in lonely exile here
   Until the Son of God appear:

   Rejoice! Rejoice! Emmanuel
   Shall come to thee, O Israel.

2 O come, thou Rod of Jesse, free
   Thine own from Satan's tyranny;
   From depths of hell thy people save,
   And give them vict'ry o'er the grave:

3 O come, thou dayspring, come and cheer
   Our spirits by thine advent here;
   Disperse the gloomy clouds of night,
   And death's dark shadows put to flight:

4 O come, thou key of David, come
   And open wide our heavenly home;
   Make safe the way that leads on high,
   And close the path to misery:

5 O come, O come, thou Lord of might,
   Who to thy tribes on Sinai's height
   In ancient times didst give the Law
   In cloud and majesty and awe:

Translated by John Mason Neale, 1818-1866

KING JESUS HATH A GARDEN

Lyrical, flowing

DUTCH, SEVENTEENTH CENTURY, ARR. M.W.

King Je-sus hath a gar-den, full of di-vers flow'rs, Where

I go cull-ing po-sies gay, all times __ and hours. There

naught is heard but Pa-ra-dise bird, Harp dul-ci-mer, lute, With cym-bal, __

trump and tym-bal, And the ten-der, sooth-ing flute; With cym-bal __

trump and tym-bal, And the ten-der, sooth-ing flute. __

KING JESUS HATH A GARDEN

Heer Jesus heeft een Hofken

1 King Jesus hath a garden, full of divers flowers,
Where I go culling posies gay, all times and hours.

There naught is heard but Paradise bird,
Harp, dulcimer, lute,
With cymbal, trump and tymbal,
And the tender, soothing flute.

2 The Lily, white in blossom there, is Chastity:
The Violet, with sweet perfume, Humanity.

There naught is heard, etc.

3 The bonny Damask-rose is known as Patïence:
The blithe and thrifty Marygold, Obedïence.

There naught is heard, etc.

4 The Crown Imperial bloometh too in yonder place,
'Tis Charity, of stock divine, the flower of grace.

There naught is heard, etc.

5 Yet, 'mid the brave, the bravest prize of all may claim
The Star of Bethlem—Jesus—blessèd be his Name!

There naught is heard, etc.

6 Ah! Jesu Lord, my heal and weal, my bliss complete,
Make thou my heart thy garden-plot, fair, trim and neat.

That I may hear this musick clear:
Harp, dulcimer, lute, etc.

Traditional Dutch from Geestlijcke Harmonie, *1633*
Translated by George Ratcliffe Woodward, 1848-1934

THE CHERRY TREE CAROL
JOSEPH AND MARY

Moderate, flowing and flexible

KENTUCKY, TRANSCRIBED BY E.P., ARR. M.W.

1 Jo - seph was — an old man, An — old man was — he, He — mar - ried vir - gin Ma - ry, The — Queen of Ga - li - lee. 2 As Jo - seph and Ma - ry was walk - ing, Was — walk - ing one — day, 'Here are ap - ples, here — are cher - ries,' So — Ma - ry did say. Then

vv 3,4,6,8

vv 5,7,9

Fine

THE CHERRY TREE CAROL
JOSEPH AND MARY

1 Joseph was an old man,
   An old man was he,
He married Virgin Mary,
   The Queen of Galilee.

2 As Joseph and Mary was walking,
   Was walking one day,
'Here are apples, here are cherries,'
   Mary did say.

3 Then Mary said to Joseph,
   So meek and so mild,
'Joseph gather me some cherries,
   For I am with child.'

4 Then Joseph flew in anger,
   In anger flew he,
'Let the father of the baby
   Gather cherries for thee.'

5 Jesus spoke a few words,
   A few words spoke he,
'Give my mother some cherries,
   Bow down, cherry tree!

6 'Bow down, cherry tree,
   Low down to the ground.'
Mary gathered cherries,
   And Joseph stood around.

7 Then Joseph took Mary
   All on his right knee,
'What have I done, Lord?
   Have mercy on me.'

8 Then Joseph took Mary
   All on his left knee,
'Oh tell me, little Baby,
   When thy birthday will be.'

9 'The sixth of January
   My birthday will be,
The stars in the elements
   Will tremble with glee.'

Transcribed from a field recording by John A. Lomax in the Archive of Folk Culture, Library of Congress, AFS 1010 A1, Joseph and Mary, sung by Jilson Setters (James W. Day) at Ashland, Kentucky, 28 June 1937

ANGELS FROM THE REALMS OF GLORY

TRADITIONAL FRENCH, ARR. E.P.

Light and lively

An - gels from the __ realms of glo - ry

Wing your __ flight o'er __ all the earth:

Ye who sang cre - a - tion's sto - ry

Now pro - claim Mes - si - ah's birth:

ANGELS FROM THE REALMS OF GLORY

1 Angels from the realms of glory
　Wing your flight o'er all the earth:
Ye who sang creation's story
　Now proclaim Messiah's birth:

　Gloria in excelsis Deo.

2 Shepherds in the field abiding,
　Watching o'er your flocks by night,
God with man is now residing;
　Yonder shines the infant Light:

3 Sages, leave your contemplations,
　Brighter visions beam afar;
Seek the great Desire of Nations,
　Ye have seen his natal star:

4 Saints before the altar bending,
　Watching long in hope and fear,
Suddenly the Lord, descending,
　In his temple shall appear:

5 Though an infant now we view him,
　He shall fill his Father's throne,
Gather all the nations round him,
　Every knee shall then bow down:

vv. 1-4 James Montgomery, 1771-1854
v. 5 anonymous, nineteenth century

SHEPHERDS! SHAKE OFF
YOUR DROWSY SLEEP

Rather fast

BESANÇON, ARR. M.W.

Shep-herds! Shake off your drow-sy sleep, Rise and

leave your sil-ly sheep; An-gels from hea-ven loud are

sing-ing; Ti-dings of great joy are bring-ing. *Shep-herds! The*

cho-rus come and swell! Sing No-el! Sing No-el!

Chantans! Bargies, Nové, Nové

1 Shepherds! Shake off your drowsy sleep,
   Rise and leave your silly sheep;
   Angels from heaven loud are singing;
   Tidings of great joy are bringing.

   Shepherds! The chorus come and swell!
   Sing Noel! Sing Noel!

2 Hark! Even now the bells ring round,
   Listen to their merry sound;
   Hark! How the birds new songs are making
   As if the winter's chains were breaking.

3 See how the flowers all burst anew,
   Thinking snow is summer dew;
   See how the stars afresh are glowing,
   All their brightest beams bestowing.

4 Cometh at length the age of peace,
   Strife and sorrow now shall cease;
   Prophets foretold the wondrous story
   Of this Heaven-born Prince of Glory.

5 Shepherds! Then up and quick away,
   Seek the Babe ere break of day;
   He is the hope of every nation,
   All in him shall find salvation.

Anonymous French

THIS ENDRIS NIGHT

With a gentle swing

ENGLISH, FIFTEENTH CENTURY, ARR. E.P.

This end - ris night I saw __ a sight, A

star as bright __ as day: _____ And e - ver a - mong, A

mai - den sung, 'Lul - lay, by, by, lul __ lay.' _____

This tune is sung twice from verse 2.

2 This lovely lady sat and sung,
    And to her child did say:
'My son, my brother, father, dear,
    Why liest thou thus in hay?
My sweetest bird, thus 'tis required,
    Though thou be king veray;
But nevertheless I will not cease
    To sing, by, by, lullay.'

3 The child then spake in his talking,
    And to his mother said:
'Yea, I am known as heaven-king,
    In crib though I be laid;
For angels bright down to me light:
    Thou knowest 'tis no nay:
And for that sight thou may'st delight
    To sing, by, by, lullay.'

4 'Now sweet son, since thou art a king,
    Why art thou laid in stall?
Why doest not order thy bedding
    In some great kingès hall?
Methinks 'tis right that king or knight
    Should lie in good array:
And then among, it were no wrong
    To sing, by, by, lullay.'

5 'Mary-mother, I am thy child,
    Though I be laid in stall;
For lords and dukes shall worship me,
    And so shall kingès all.

Ye shall well see that Kingès three
    Shall come on this twelfth day,
For this behest, give me thy breast,
    And sing, by, by, lullay.'

6 'Now tell, sweet son, I thee do pray,
    Thou art my love and dear –
How should I keep thee to thy pay,
    And make thee glad of cheer?
For all thy will I would fulfil –
    Thou knowest well, in fay;
And for all this I will thee kiss,
    And sing, by, by, lullay.'

7 'My dear mother, when time it be,
    Take thou me up on loft,
And set me then upon thy knee,
    And handle me full soft;
And in thy arm thou hold me warm,
    And keep me night and day,
And if I weep, and may not sleep,
    Thou sing, by, by, lullay.'

8 'Now sweet son, since it is come so,
    That all is at thy will,
I pray thee grant to me a boon,
    If it be right and skill –
That child or man, who will or can
    Be merry on my day,
To bliss thou bring – and I shall sing,
    Lullay, by, by, lullay.'

Anonymous English, fifteenth century

LITTLE CHILD THERE IS YBORE

GERMAN, SIXTEENTH CENTURY, ARR. E.P.

Flowing, with a broad swing

A lit - tle child there is ___ y - bore E-
- ia, E - ia, su - san - ni, su - san - ni,
su - san - ni, Y - sprung - en out of Jes - se's
more, Al - le - lu - ia. Al - le - lu -
- ia, To save ___ us all ___ that were fore - lore.

A LITTLE CHILD THERE IS YBORE

1 A little child there is ybore,
Eia, Eia, susanni,* susanni, susanni,
Ysprungen out of Jesse's more,†
Alleluia, Alleluia,
To save us all that were forlore.

2 Jesus that is so full of might
Ybore he was about midnight;
The angels sung with all their might.

3 Jesus is that childës name,
A maid and mother is his dame,
And so our sorrow is turned to game.

4 Three kings there came with their presents
Of myrrh and gold and frankincense,
As clerkës sing in their sequence.

5 Now sit we down upon our knee,
And pray that child that is so free:
And with good heartë now sing we.

*English (without Latin refrain) in Bodleian Library,
Oxford, MS. Ashmole 1393, fo. 69 v.*

* *Susanni:* from German lulling words
† *More,* stock

O JESU, SWEET CHILD

SAMUEL SCHEIDT, 1587-1654, HARMONIZED BY
J.S. BACH, ADAPTED BY M.W.

O Je - su, sweet child, O Je - su so

mild, The Fa - ther's will hast

thou ___ ful - filled; Thou cam'st from

hea - ven for our sake, Our frail hu -

- ma - ni - ty to take, O Je - su, sweet

child, O Je - su so mild.

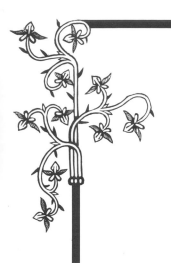

O JESU, SWEET CHILD

O Jesulein süss

1 O Jesu, sweet child, O Jesu so mild,
  The Father's will hast thou fulfilled;
  Thou cam'st from heaven for our sake,
  Our frail humanity to take,
  O Jesu, sweet child, O Jesu so mild.

2 O Jesu, sweet child, O Jesu so mild Jesu so mild,
  The world with gladness thou hast filled;
  Thou cam'st to earth from heaven's height,
  With comfort in our bitter plight,
  O Jesu, sweet child, O Jesu so mild.

3 O Jesu, sweet child, O Jesu so mild,
  Love's image, thou, all undefiled;
  Inflame our hearts with love's sweet fire,
  That love of thee be our desire,
  O Jesu, sweet child, O Jesu so mild.

4 O Jesu, sweet child, O Jesu so mild.
  Help us to do as thou hast willed;
  For all we have is thine alone,
  O guide us, keep us for thine own,
  O Jesu, sweet child, O Jesu so mild.

Samuel Scheidt, 1587-1654
Translated by Elizabeth
Poston, 1905-1987 and
Malcolm Williamson, b.1931

41

DECK THE HALL

TRADITIONAL WELSH, ARR. M.W.

Fast and joyous

Deck the hall with boughs of hol - ly, Fa la la la la, la

la la la, 'Tis the sea - son to be jol - ly,

Fa la la la la, la la la la; Don we now our

best ap - pa - rel, Fa la la, la la la, la la la,

Troll the an - cient Christ - mas ca - rol,

Fa la la la la, la la la la.

2 See the blazing log before us, *Fa la la, etc.,*
Strike the harp and join the chorus,
Follow me in merry measure,
While I tell of Christmas treasure,

3 Fast away the old year passes, *Fa la la, etc.,*
Hail the new year, lads and lasses,
Sing we joyously together,
Heedless of the wind and weather,

Traditional Welsh

THE BOAR'S HEAD CAROL

At a moderate speed, broad and steady

TRADITIONAL ENGLISH, ARR. E.P.

The boar's head in hand bear I, Be-
The boar's head, as I un-der-stand, Is the

-decked with bays and rose-ma-ry: And I pray you, my mas-ters,
ra-rest dish in all the land, When thus be-decked with a

be mer-ry, *Quot es-tis in con-vi-vi-o:*
gay gar-land, *Let us ser-vi-re can-ti-co:*

Ca-put a-pri de-fe-ro. Red-dens lau-des Do-mi-no.

1 The boar's head in hand bear I,
Bedecked with bays and rosemary;
And I pray you, my masters, be merry,

  Quot estis in convivio:
  Caput apri defero,
  *Reddens laudes Domino.**

2 The boar's head, as I understand,
Is the rarest dish in all the land
When thus bedecked with a gay garland,

  Let us *servire cantico:*†
  Caput apri defero,
  Reddens laudes Domino.

3 Our steward hath provided this
In honour of the King of bliss,
Which on this day to be servèd is,

  In Reginensi atrio:‡
  Caput apri defero,
  Reddens laudes Domino.

Queen's College, Oxford, version

* *Quot, etc.* So many as are in the feast:
  The boar's head I bring,
  Giving praises to the Lord.
† *Servire, etc.* Let us serve with a song:
‡ *In, etc.* In the Queen's hall:

43

IN THE BLEAK MID-WINTER

In moderate time

GUSTAV HOLST, 1874-1934, ADAPTED BY M.W.

In the bleak mid - win - ter Fros - ty wind made moan, Earth stood hard as ir - on, Wa - ter like a stone; Snow had fal - len, snow on snow, Snow ___ on ___ snow, In the bleak mid - win - ter, Long ___ a - go.

IN THE BLEAK MID-WINTER

1 In the bleak mid-winter
   Frosty wind made moan,
Earth stood hard as iron,
   Water like a stone;
Snow had fallen, snow on snow,
   Snow on snow,
In the bleak mid-winter,
   Long ago.

2 Our God, heaven cannot hold him
   Nor earth sustain;
Heaven and earth shall flee away
   When he comes to reign:
In the bleak mid-winter
   A stable-place sufficed
The Lord God Almighty,
   Jesus Christ.

3 Enough for him, whom cherubim
   Worship night and day,
A breastful of milk,
   And a mangerful of hay;
Enough for him, whom angels
   Fall down before,
The ox and ass and camel
   Which adore.

4 Angels and archangels
   May have gathered there,
Cherubim and seraphim
   Thronged the air:
But only his mother
   In her maiden bliss
Worshipped the Belovèd
   With a kiss.

5 What can I give him,
   Poor as I am?
If I were a shepherd
   I would bring a lamb;
If I were a wise man
   I would do my part;
Yet what I can I give him –
   Give my heart.

Christina Rossetti, 1830-1894

HARK! THE HERALD ANGELS SING

FELIX MENDELSSOHN-BARTHOLDY, 1809-1847,
ADAPTED BY W.H. CUMMINGS, 1831-1915, ARR. E.P.

Moderately fast

Hark! the he - rald an - gels sing _ Glo - ry to the new-born King: Peace on earth and mer-cy mild, _ God and sin - ners re - con - ciled: Joy - ful, all ye na - tions, rise, _ Join the tri - umph of the skies, _ with the an - ge - lic host pro - claim Christ is _ born in Beth - le - hem! *Hark! the he - rald an - gels sing, 'Glo - ry _ to the new-born King.'*

HARK! THE HERALD ANGELS SING

1 Hark! the herald angels sing
Glory to the new-born King;
Peace on earth and mercy mild,
God and sinners reconciled:
Joyful, all ye nations, rise,
Join the triumph of the skies,
With the angelic host proclaim
Christ is born in Bethlehem!

Hark! the herald angels sing,
'Glory to the new-born King'.

2 Christ, by highest heaven adored,
Christ, the everlasting Lord,
Late in time behold him come,
Offspring of a Virgin's womb;
Veiled in flesh the Godhead see,
Hail the incarnate Deity!
Pleased as man with man to dwell,
Jesus, our Emmanuel:

3 Hail the heaven-born Prince of Peace!
Hail the Sun of Righteousness!
Light and life to all he brings,
Risen with healing in his wings;
Mild he lays his glory by,
Born that man no more may die,
Born to raise the sons of earth,
Born to give them second birth:

Charles Wesley, 1707-1788
George Whitefield, 1714-1770
Martin Madan, 1726-1790

ON CHRISTMAS NIGHT

Fast and loud

TRADITIONAL SUSSEX, ARR. M.W.

On Christ-mas night all Christ-ians sing To

hear the news __ the an-gels bring. On Christ-mas night all

Christ-ians sing to hear the news __ the an - gels bring —

News of great joy, __ news of __ great mirth,

News of our mer-ci-ful __ King's birth. __

1 On Christmas night all Christians sing
To hear the news the angels bring –
News of great joy, news of great mirth,
News of our merciful King's birth.

2 Then why should men on earth be so sad,
Since our Redeemer made us glad?
When from our sin he set us free,
All for to gain our liberty.

3 When sin departs before his grace,
Then life and health come in its place;
Angels and men with joy may sing,
All for to see the new-born King.

4 All out of darkness we have light,
Which made the angels sing this night;
'Glory to God and peace to men,
Now and for evermore. Amen.'

Traditional English
Tune and text collected by
Ralph Vaughan Williams, 1872-1958

48

SHEPHERDS' ROCKING CAROL

Smooth and gentle

TRADITIONAL CZECH, ARR. M.W.

Hush you, Je-sus, ba-by King, ba-by King,

See a coat of fur we bring

We will rock you, hush you, wrap you, That sweet sleep may

warm - ly lap you; Hush you, dar - ling

lit - tle one, Ma-ry's ba - by, Ma-ry's son.

Hajej, Nynej

Hush you, Jesus, baby King,
See, a coat of fur we bring.
We will rock you, hush you, wrap you,
That sweet sleep may warmly lap you;
Hush you, darling little one,
Mary's baby, Mary's son.

Traditional Czech
Translated by Elizabeth Poston, 1905-1987

Silent Night

Gentle and smooth

FRANZ GRÜBER, 1787-1863, ARR. E.P.

Si - lent night, ho - ly night, Still the earth,

lone the light Where in Beth - le - hem Watch the blest pair.

Cur - ly haired In - fant so ten - der and fair, Sleep in hea - ven - ly

peace, _____ Sleep __ in hea - ven - ly peace.

SILENT NIGHT

Still Nacht! heilige Nacht!

1 Silent night, holy night,
   Still the earth, lone the light
   Where in Bethlehem watch the blest pair.
   Curly haired Infant so tender and fair,
   Sleep in heavenly peace,
   Sleep in heavenly peace.

2 Silent night, holy night,
   Shepherds, hushed, saw the sight,
   Heard the angelic Alleluia
   Ring, proclaiming from far and near,
   Christ the Saviour is here,
   Christ the Saviour is here.

3 Silent night, holy night,
   Holy Babe, smiles alight,
   Radiant, from thy innocent face,
   In this saving hour of thy grace,
   Christ, our Lord, at thy birth,
   Christ, our Lord, at thy birth.

Joseph Mohr, 1792-1848, written 1818
Translated by Elizabeth Poston, 1905-1987

MASTERS IN THIS HALL

FRENCH, ARR. M.W.

Ma - sters in this Hall, _____ Hear ye news to -

- day, _____ Brought from o - ver -

- sea, _____ And e - ver I you pray:

Refrain

Now - ell! Now - ell! Now - ell!

1. Now - ell sing we
2. Now - ell sing we

clear! Holp - en are all folk on earth, ___ Born ___
loud! God to - day hath poor folk raised ___ And ___

(1) is God's son so dear: (2) cast a - down the proud.

MASTERS IN THIS HALL

1 Masters in this Hall,
     Hear ye news to-day
  Brought from over sea,
     And ever I you pray:

    Nowell! Nowell! Nowell!
    Nowell sing we clear!
    Holpen are all folk on earth,
    Born is God's son so dear:
    Nowell! Nowell! Nowell!
    Nowell sing we loud!
    God to-day hath poor folk raised
    And cast a-down the proud.

2 Going o'er the hills,
     Through the milk-white snow,
  Heard I ewes bleat
     While the wind did blow:

3 Shepherds many an one
     Sat among the sheep,
  No man spake more word
     Than they had been asleep:

4 Quoth I, 'Fellows mine,
     Why this guise sit ye?
  Making but dull cheer,
     Shepherds though ye be?'

5 'Shepherds should of right
     Leap and dance and sing,
  Thus to see ye sit,
     Is a right strange thing':

6 Quoth these fellows then,
     'To Bethlem town we go,
  To see a mighty lord
     Lie in manger low':

7 'How name ye this lord,
     Shepherds?' then said I,
  'Very God,' they said,
     'Come from Heaven high':

8 Then to Bethlem town
     We went two and two,
  And in a sorry place
     Heard the oxen low:

9 Therein did we see
     A sweet and goodly may
  And a fair old man,
     Upon the straw she lay:

10 And a little child
     On her arm had she,
  'Wot ye who this is?'
     Said the hinds to me:

11 Ox and ass him know,
     Kneeling on their knee,
  Wondrous joy had I
     This little babe to see:

12 This is Christ the Lord,
     Masters be ye glad!
  Christmas is come in,
     And no folk should be sad:

William Morris, 1834-1896

CHILD IN THE MANGER

CHILD IN THE MANGER

1 Child in the manger, Infant of Mary;
   Outcast and stranger, Lord of all;
   Child who inherits all our transgressions,
   All our demerits on him fall.

2 Once the most holy Child of salvation
   Gently and lowly lived below;
   Now as our glorious mighty Redeemer,
   See him victorious o'er each foe.

3 Prophets foretold him, Infant of wonder;
   Angels behold him on his throne;
   Worthy our Saviour of all our praises;
   Happy forever are his own.

Mary Macdonald, 1817-1890
Translated by Lachlan Macbean, 1853-1931

PERSONENT HODIE
THE BOYS' CAROL

FOURTEENTH-CENTURY TUNE,
PIAE CANTIONES, 1582, ARR. M.W.

At a brisk pace, strongly rhythmical

Let the boys' cheer - ful noise Sing to - day

none but joys, Praise a - loud, clear and proud,

Praise to him in cho - rus, Giv'n from hea - ven

for us, Vir - gin - born, born, born,

Vir - gin - born, born, born, Vir - gin - born

on that morn, pro - cre - at - ed for us.

PERSONENT HODIE
THE BOYS' CAROL

1 Let the boys' cheerful noise
  Sing today none but joys,
  Praise aloud, clear and proud,
  Praise to him in chorus,
  Giv'n from heaven for us,
    Virgin-born, born, born,
    Virgin-born, born, born,
  Virgin-born on that morn, procreated for us.

2 He who rules heaven and earth
  Lies in stall at his birth,
  Humble beasts at his feast
  See the Light eternal
  Vanquish realms infernal:
    Satan's done, done, done,
    Satan's done, done, done,
  Satan's done, God has won, victor, he, supernal.

3 Magi come from afar
  See their sun, tiny one,
  Follow far little star,
  At the crib adoring,
  Man to God restoring,
    Gold and myrrh, myrrh, myrrh,
    Gold and myrrh, myrrh, myrrh,
  Gold and myrrh offered there, incense for adoring.

4 Clerk and boy, join in joy,
  Sing as heaven sings for joy,
  God this day here doth stay,
  Pour we forth the story
  Of his might and glory:
    So to God, God, God,
    So to God, God, God,
  So to God glory be, in the highest, glory.

Piae Cantiones, 1582
Translated by Elizabeth Poston, 1905-1987

JESUS CHRIST THE APPLE TREE

In moderate time

ELIZABETH POSTON, 1905-1987

The tree of life my soul hath seen, La-den with fruit and al-ways green: The tree of life my soul hath seen, La-den with fruit and al-ways green: The trees of na-ture fruit-less be Com-pared with Christ the ap-ple tree.

1 The tree of life my soul hath seen,
  Laden with fruit and always green:
  The trees of nature fruitless be
  Compared with Christ the apple tree.

JESUS CHRIST THE APPLE TREE

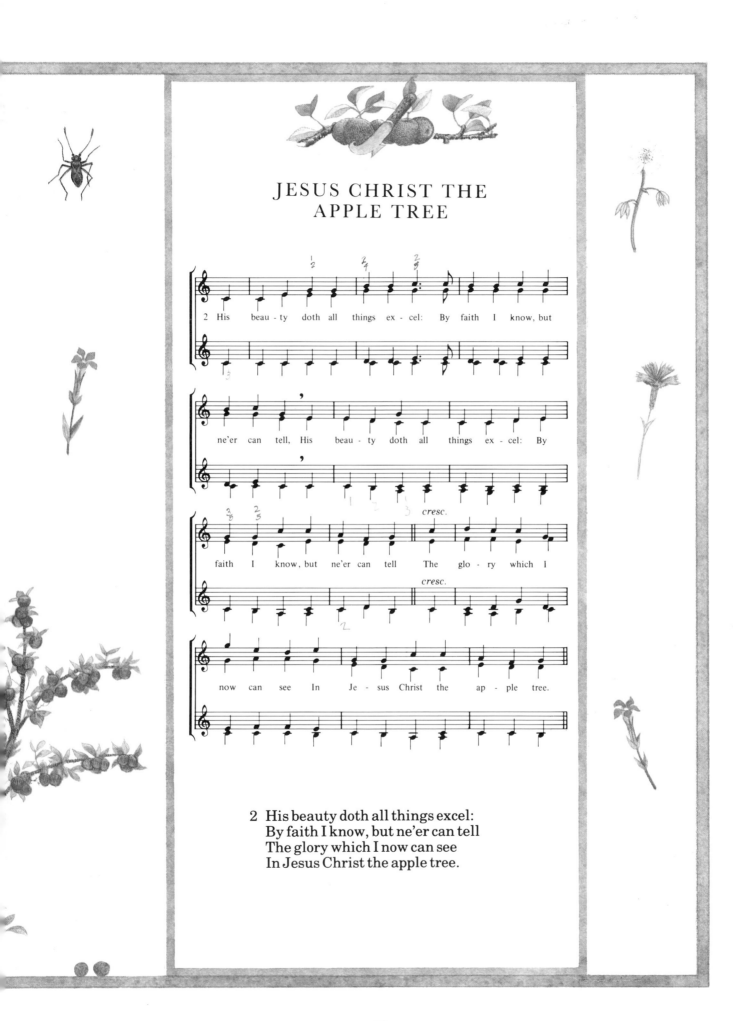

2 His beauty doth all things excel:
By faith I know, but ne'er can tell
The glory which I now can see
In Jesus Christ the apple tree.

JESUS CHRIST THE
APPLE TREE

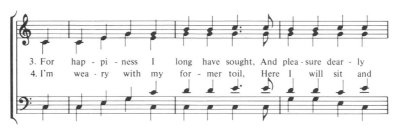

3. For hap-pi-ness I long have sought, And plea-sure dear-ly
4. I'm wea-ry with my for-mer toil, Here I will sit and

I have bought: For hap-pi-ness I long have sought, and
rest a-while: I'm wea-ry with my for-mer toil, Here

plea-sure dear-ly I have bought: I missed of all; but
I will sit and rest a-while: Un-der the sha-dow

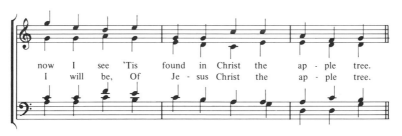

now I see 'Tis found in Christ the ap-ple tree.
I will be, Of Je-sus Christ the ap-ple tree.

3   For happiness I long have sought,
     And pleasure dearly I have bought:
     I missed of all; but now I see
     'Tis found in Christ the apple tree.

4   I'm weary with my former toil,
     Here I will sit and rest awhile:
     Under the shadow I will be,
     Of Jesus Christ the apple tree.

JESUS CHRIST THE
APPLE TREE

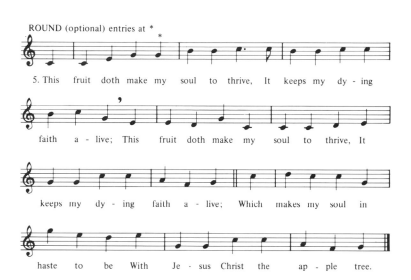

ROUND (optional) entries at *

5. This fruit doth make my soul to thrive, It keeps my dy - ing

faith a - live; This fruit doth make my soul to thrive, It

keeps my dy - ing faith a - live; Which makes my soul in

haste to be With Je - sus Christ the ap - ple tree.

5   This fruit doth make my soul to thrive,
    It keeps my dying faith alive;
    Which makes my soul in haste to be
    With Jesus Christ the apple tree.

*Divine Hymns or Spiritual Songs,
compiled by Joshua Smith,
New Hampshire, 1784*

O CHRISTMAS TREE

O Tannenbaum, O Tannenbaum!

1 O Christmas tree, O Christmas tree!
Thou tree most fair and lovely!
O Christmas tree, O Christmas tree!
Thou tree most fair and lovely!
The sight of thee at Christmastide
Spreads hope and gladness far and wide.
O Christmas tree, O Christmas tree!
Thou tree most fair and lovely!

2 O Christmas tree, O Christmas tree!
Thou hast a wondrous message.
O Christmas tree, O Christmas tree!
Thou hast a wondrous message.
Thou dost proclaim the Saviour's birth,
Goodwill to men and peace on earth.
O Christmas tree, O Christmas tree!
Thou hast a wondrous message.

Ernst G. Anschütz, written 1824

UNTO US IS BORN A SON

Brisk and vigorous   GERMAN, FIFTEENTH CENTURY, ARR. E.P.

Un - to us is born a son, King of choirs su -

- per - nal: See on earth his life be - gun, Of lords the Lord e -

- ter - nal, Of lords the Lord e - ter - nal.

Puer nobis nascitur

1 Unto us is born a son,
　　King of choirs supernal:
　See on earth his life begun,
　　Of lords the Lord eternal.

2 Christ, from heav'n descending low,
　　Comes on earth a stranger;
　Ox and ass their Owner know
　　Now cradled in a manger.

3 This did Herod sore affray,
　　And did him bewilder,
　So he gave the word to slay,
　　And slew the little childer.

4 Of his love and mercy mild
　　Hear the Christmas story:
　O that Mary's gentle Child
　　Might lead us up to glory!

5 O and A and A and O,
　　Cantemus in choro,
　Voice and organ, sing we so,
　　Benedicamus Domino.

*Fifteenth century, adapted from the translation
by George Ratcliffe Woodward, 1859-1934*

63

IT CAME UPON THE
MIDNIGHT CLEAR

Moderate

TRADITIONAL ENGLISH, ARR. M.W.

It came up-on the __ mid-night clear, That glo-rious song __ of old, From __ an-gels bend-ing near the earth To __ touch __ their harps of gold: 'Peace on the earth, good-will to men, From heaven's all - gra-cious King!' The world in so-lemn __ still - ness lay To __ hear __ the an-gels sing.

IT CAME UPON THE
MIDNIGHT CLEAR

1 It came upon the midnight clear,
    That glorious song of old,
From angels bending near the earth
    To touch their harps of gold:
'Peace on the earth, goodwill to men,
    From heaven's all-gracious King!'
The world in solemn stillness lay
    To hear the angels sing.

2 Still through the cloven skies they come,
    With peaceful wings unfurled;
And still their heavenly music floats
    O'er all the weary world;
Above its sad and lowly plains
    They bend on hovering wing;
And ever o'er its Babel sounds
    The blessèd angels sing.

3 Yet with the woes of sin and strife
    The world has suffered long;
Beneath the angel-strain have rolled
    Two thousand years of wrong;
And man, at war with man, hears not
    The love-song which they bring;
O hush the noise, ye men of strife,
    And hear the angels sing.

4 And ye, beneath life's crushing load,
    Whose forms are bending low,
Who toil along the climbing way
    With painful steps and slow,
Take heart, for comfort, love, and hope
    Come swiftly on the wing;
O rest beside the weary road,
    And hear the angels sing.

5 For lo, the days are hastening on,
    That prophets knew of old,
And with the ever-circling years
    Comes round the day foretold.
May peace on earth in every land
    Its joy and healing bring,
And the whole world send back the song
    Which now the angels sing.

Edmund Hamilton Sears, 1810-1876 (the last verse adapted)

WHILE SHEPHERDS WATCHED THEIR FLOCKS BY NIGHT

Rather animated

ESTE'S *PSALTER*, 1592, ARR. E.P.

While shep-herds watched their flocks by night, All sea-ted on the ground, The an-gel of the Lord came down, And glo-ry shone a-round.

WHILE SHEPHERDS WATCHED THEIR FLOCKS BY NIGHT

1 While shepherds watched their flocks by night,
    All seated on the ground,
The angel of the Lord came down,
    And glory shone around.

2 'Fear not,' said he (for mighty dread
    Had seized their troubled mind);
'Glad tidings of great joy I bring
    To you and all mankind.

3 'To you in David's town this day
    Is born of David's line
A Saviour, who is Christ the Lord;
    And this shall be the sign:

4 'The heavenly babe you there shall find
    To human view displayed,
All meanly wrapped in swathing[1] bands
    And in a manger laid.'

5 Thus spake the seraph; and forthwith
    Appeared a shining throng
Of angels praising God, who thus
    Addressed their joyful song:

6 'All glory be to God on high,
    And to the earth be peace;
Goodwill henceforth from heaven to men
    Begin and never cease.'

Nahum Tate, 1652-1715

[1] Pronounce 'swaything'

O LITTLE TOWN OF
BETHLEHEM

TRADITIONAL ENGLISH, ARR. M.W.

Moderate

O lit - tle town of Beth - le - hem, How still we __ see thee lie! A - bove thy deep and dream - less __ sleep The si - lent __ stars go by. Yet __ in thy dark __ streets __ shi - - neth The e - ver - last - ing light; The hopes and fears of all __ the __ years Are met in __ thee to - night.

O LITTLE TOWN OF BETHLEHEM

1 O little town of Bethlehem,
    How still we see thee lie!
Above thy deep and dreamless sleep
    The silent stars go by.
Yet in thy dark streets shineth
    The everlasting light;
The hopes and fears of all the years
    Are met in thee tonight.

2 O morning stars, together
    Proclaim the holy birth,
And praises sing to God the King,
    And peace to men on earth;
For Christ is born of Mary;
    And, gathered all above,
While mortals sleep, the angels keep
    Their watch of wondering love.

3 How silently, how silently,
    The wondrous gift is given!
So God imparts to human hearts
    The blessings of his heaven.
No ear may hear his coming;
    But in this world of sin,
Where meek souls will receive him, still
    The dear Christ enters in.

4 Where children pure and happy
    Pray to the blessèd Child,
Where misery cries out to thee,
    Son of the mother mild;
Where charity stands watching
    And faith holds wide the door,
The dark night wakes, the glory breaks,
    And Christmas comes once more.

5 O holy Child of Bethlehem,
    Descend to us, we pray;
Cast out our sin, and enter in,
    Be born in us today.
We hear the Christmas Angels
    The great glad tidings tell:
O come to us, abide with us,
    Our Lord Emmanuel.

Bishop Phillips Brooks, 1835-1893

AWAY IN A MANGER

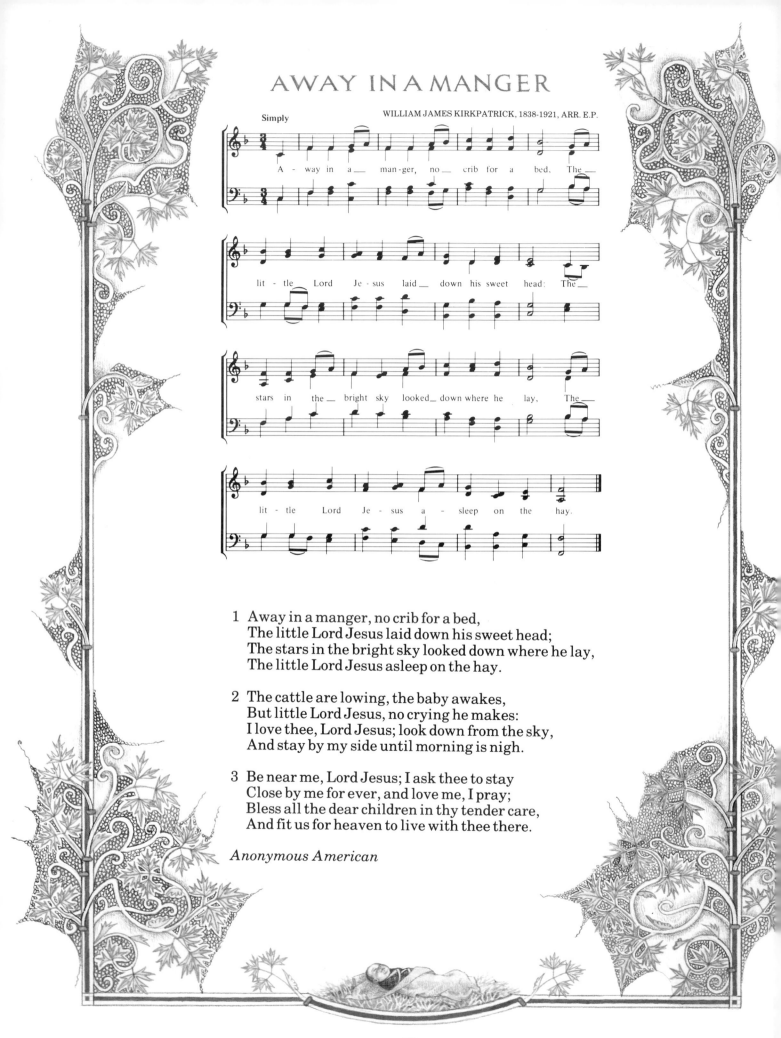

1 Away in a manger, no crib for a bed,
   The little Lord Jesus laid down his sweet head;
   The stars in the bright sky looked down where he lay,
   The little Lord Jesus asleep on the hay.

2 The cattle are lowing, the baby awakes,
   But little Lord Jesus, no crying he makes:
   I love thee, Lord Jesus; look down from the sky,
   And stay by my side until morning is nigh.

3 Be near me, Lord Jesus; I ask thee to stay
   Close by me for ever, and love me, I pray;
   Bless all the dear children in thy tender care,
   And fit us for heaven to live with thee there.

Anonymous American

SHEEP AND SHEPHERDS

Quem pastores laudavere

1 Sheep and shepherds, while God praising,
Heard angelic voices raising,
Telling them of fear abated
At the King of glory's birth.

2 Wise men through the night were faring
To the crib of glory, bearing
Gifts of love all immolated
To the King of glory's birth.

3 We to God all praise are singing,
Thanks to Mary, upward winging;
So may God be venerated
For the King of heaven's birth.

Translated by Malcolm Williamson, b.1931

SEE AMID THE WINTER'S SNOW

Contemplative but flowing

JOHN GOSS, 1800-1880, ARR. M.W.

See, a-mid the win-ter's snow, Born for us on earth be-low, See, the ten-der Lamb ap-pears, Prom-ised from e-ter-nal years.

Hail, thou e-ver bless-ed morn! Hail re-demp-tion's hap-py dawn! Sing through all Je-ru-sa-lem, Christ is born in Beth-le-hem.

SEE AMID THE WINTER'S SNOW

1 See amid the winter's snow,
  Born for us on earth below,
  See the tender Lamb appears,
  Promised from eternal years.

    Hail, thou ever-blessèd morn;
    Hail, redemption's happy dawn!
    Sing through all Jerusalem,
    Christ is born in Bethlehem.

2 Lo, within a manger lies
  He who built the starry skies;
  He who throned in height sublime
  Sits amid the cherubim.

3 Say, ye holy shepherds, say
  What your joyful news today;
  Wherefore have ye left your sheep
  On the lonely mountain steep?

4 'As we watched at dead of night,
  Lo, we saw a wondrous light;
  Angels singing "Peace on earth"
  Told us of the Saviour's birth'.

5 Sacred infant, all divine,
  What a tender love was thine,
  Thus to come from highest bliss
  Down to such a world as this.

Edward Caswall, 1814-1878

COVENTRY CAROL

Lully, lulla, thou little tiny child;
By, by, lully, lullay.

1 O sisters two,
  How may we do
    For to preserve this day
  This poor youngling
  For whom we do sing
    By, by, lully lullay?

2 Herod the king,
  In his raging,
    Chargèd he hath this day
  His men of might,
  In his own sight
    All young children to slay.

3 That woe is me,
  Poor child, for thee,
    And ever mourn and say:
  For thy parting
  Neither say nor sing
    By, by, lully lullay.

Pageant of the Shearmen and Tailors
Traditional English

AS WITH GLADNESS MEN OF OLD

CHORALE BY KONRAD KOCHER, 1786-1872,
ADAPTED BY M.W.

Stately, but not too slow

As with gladness men of old Did the guiding
star be - hold, As with joy they hailed its light,
Lead - ing on - ward, beam - ing bright: So, most gra - cious
Lord, may we E - ver - more be led to thee.

AS WITH GLADNESS MEN
OF OLD

1 As with gladness men of old
  Did the guiding star behold,
  As with joy they hailed its light,
  Leading onward, beaming bright:
  So, most gracious Lord, may we
  Evermore be led to thee.

2 As with joyful steps they sped,
  To that lowly manger-bed,
  There to bend the knee before
  Him whom heaven and earth adore,
  So may we with willing feet
  Ever seek thy mercy-seat.

3 As they offered gifts most rare
  At that manger rude and bare,
  So may we with holy joy,
  Pure, and free from sin's alloy,
  All our costliest treasures bring,
  Christ, to thee our heavenly King.

4 Holy Jesu, every day
  Keep us in the narrow way;
  And, when earthly things are past,
  Bring our ransomed souls at last
  Where they need no star to guide,
  Where no clouds thy glory hide.

5 In the heavenly country bright
  Need they no created light;
  Thou its Light, its Joy, its Crown,
  Thou its Sun which goes not down:
  There for ever may we sing
  Alleluyas to our King.

William Chatterton Dix, 1837-1898

THE FIRST NOWELL

TRADITIONAL ENGLISH, HARMONIZED BY
JOHN STAINER, 1840-1901, ADAPTED BY E.P.

Brisk and cheerful

The first __ Now-ell the __ an-gel did say Was to

cer-tain poor shep-herds in fields as they lay: In __ fields __ where __

they lay __ keep-ing their sheep, In a cold win-ter's night __ that

was __ so deep: Now - ell, __ Now - ell, Now - ell, Now -

- ell, Born is the King __ of Is - ra - el.

THE FIRST NOWELL

1 The first Nowell the angel did say
  Was to certain poor shepherds in fields as they lay;
  In fields where they lay keeping their sheep,
  In a cold winter's night that was so deep:

Nowell, Nowell, Nowell, Nowell,
Born is the King of Israel.

2 They lookèd up and saw a star,
  Shining in the east, beyond them far;
  And to the earth it gave great light,
  And it continued both day and night:

3 And by the light of that same star,
  Three Wise Men came from country far;
  To seek for a king was their intent,
  And to follow the star wheresoever it went:

4 This star drew nigh to the north west;
  O'er Bethlehem it took its rest,
  And there it did both stop and stay
  Right over the place where Jesus lay:

5 Then did they know assuredly
  Within that house the King did lie:
  One entered in then for to see,
  And found the babe in poverty:

6 Then entered in those Wise Men three,
  Fell reverently upon their knee,
  And offered there in his presence
  Both gold and myrrh and frankincense:

7 Between an ox-stall and an ass
  This child truly there born he was;
  For want of clothing they did him lay
  All in a manger, among the hay:

8 Then let us all with one accord
  Sing praises to our heavenly Lord,
  That hath made heaven and earth of nought,
  And with his blood mankind hath bought:

9 If we in our time shall do well,
  We shall be free from death and hell;
  For God hath preparèd for us all
  A resting place in general:

Traditional English, from William Sandys, Christmas Carols Ancient and Modern, *1833*

COME, TUNE YOUR CHEERFUL VOICE

Lively and swinging

TRADITIONAL ENGLISH, ARR. E.P.

Come, tune your cheer-ful voice; Loud an-thems let us sing, ____ For un-to us ___ is born to-day, For un - to us ___ is born to-day A Sa - viour and a King; ____ For un-to us ___ is born to - - day ____ A Sa - viour and ___ a King, A Sa - viour and a King.

COME, TUNE YOUR
CHEERFUL VOICE

1 Come, tune your cheerful voice;
  Loud anthems let us sing,
  For unto us is born today
  A Saviour and a King.

2 Hark! What a joyful sound
  Re-echoes from above,
  The angels singing praise to God
  For his redeeming love!

3 All hail our Saviour God!
  Due thanks before him pay
  For his great mercies shown to men
  On this auspicious day.

4 'All glory be to God,'
  Aloud, let angels sing!
  For unto us is born today
  A Saviour and a King.

Traditional English

A CHILD THIS DAY IS BORN

Brisk and cheerful

TRADITIONAL ENGLISH, ARR. E.P.

A child this day is ____ born, A
Now - ell, Now - ell, Now - ell, Now -

child of high _ re - nown, Most wor - thy of _ his
- ell, sing all _ we may, Be - cause the King _ of

scep - tre, A scep - tre and a crown:
all ____ Kings Was born this bless - ed day.

1　A child this day is born,
　　　A child of high renown,
　　Most worthy of his sceptre,
　　　A sceptre and a crown:

　　　Nowell, Nowell, Nowell,
　　　　Nowell, sing all we may,
　　　Because the King of all Kings
　　　Was born this blessed day.

2　These tidings shepherds heard,
　　　In field watching their fold,
　　Were by an angel unto them
　　　That night revealed and told,

3　To whom the angel spoke,
　　　Saying, 'Be not afraid;
　　Be glad, poor silly* shepherds,
　　　Why are you so dismayed?'

4　'For lo! I bring you tidings
　　　Of gladness and of mirth,
　　Which cometh to all people by
　　　This holy infant's birth.'

5　Glory be unto our God,
　　　That sitteth still on high,
　　With praises and with triumph great,
　　　And joyful melody.

6　And as the angel told them,
　　　So to them did appear;
　　They found the young child Jesus Christ,
　　　With Mary his mother dear.

Traditional English

* *Silly,* blessed (selig).

JOY TO THE WORLD

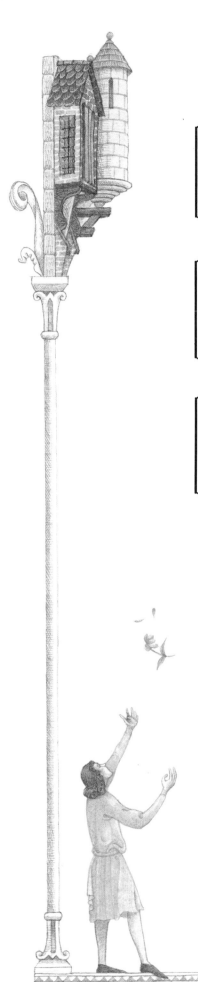

With measured tread

NICOLAUS HERMANN, 1485-1561, ARR. M.W.

Joy to the world! The Lord is come: Let earth re-ceive her

King, Let ev'-ry heart pre-pare him room, And

heaven and na-ture sing, _____ And heaven and na-ture sing.

1 Joy to the world! The Lord is come:
  Let earth receive her King,
  Let every heart prepare him room,
  And heaven and nature sing.

2 Joy to the earth! The Saviour reigns:
  Let men their songs employ;
  While fields and floods, rocks, hills and plains
  Repeat the sounding joy.

3 No more let sin and sorrow grow,
  Nor thorns infest the ground:
  He comes to make his blessings flow
  Far as the curse is found.

4 He rules the world with truth and grace,
  And makes the nations prove
  The glories of his righteousness
  And wonders of his love.

Isaac Watts, 1674-1748

IN DULCI JUBILO

Moderate, with a gentle lilt

GERMAN, FOURTEENTH CENTURY, ARR. E.P.

In dul - ci ju - bi - lo ___ Now sing we all I -

-O, I - O, Our most pre - cious trea - sure Lies

in prae - se - pi - o ___ And as the sun He

shi - neth Ma - tris in gre - mi - o: ___

Al - pha es et O! ___ *Al - pha es et O!* ___

84

IN DULCI JUBILO

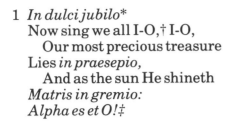

1 *In dulci jubilo**
  Now sing we all I-O,† I-O,
    Our most precious treasure
  Lies *in praesepio*,
    And as the sun He shineth
  Matris in gremio:
  Alpha es et O!‡

2 *O Jesu, parvule,*
  My heart grieves sore for thee;
    Comfort all my sadness,
  O puer optime,
    And with thy holy gladness,
  O princeps gloriae,
  Trahe me post te!

3 *O Patris caritas!*
  O Nati lenitas!
    We were deeply stainèd
  Per nostra crimina;
    But thou for us hast gainèd
  Coelorum gaudia,
  O qualis gloria!

4 *Ubi sunt gaudia?*
  O nowhere more than here;
    Angels there are singing
  Nova cantica,
    There the bells are ringing
  In Regis curia,
  O that we were there!

*Fourteenth-century German/Latin
macaronic carol, German translation
by Elizabeth Poston, 1905-1987*

1 *In dulci jubilo*
  Now sing we all I-O, I-O,
    Our most precious treasure
  Lies in a stable's glow,
    And as the sun He shineth
  Mary's Babe reclineth:
  Alpha es et O!

2 O Jesu, tiny son,
  My heart grieves sore for thee;
    Comfort all my sadness,
  O thou most gracious boy,
    And with thy holy gladness,
  O Prince of Glory, hear me,
  Draw me unto thee!

3 O kindness of the Father!
  O mildness of the Son!
    We were deeply stainèd
  By all our sin and shame;
    But thou for us hast gainèd
  The bliss of Heaven's name.
  O what joy is there!

4 Seek we joy now where?
  O nowhere more than here;
    Angels there are singing
  Songs both new and rare,
    There the bells are ringing
  In Heaven's court so fair.
  O that we were there!

*Alternative English version
by Elizabeth Poston, 1905-1987*

* *With a sweet shout of joy*
† *Exclamation of joy from the Greek*
‡ *Thou art Alpha and Omega – the first and last letters of the Greek alphabet*

AS I SAT ON A SUNNY BANK

1 As I sat on a sunny bank, a sunny bank, a sunny bank,
   As I sat on a sunny bank

   On Christmas Day in the morning.

2 I saw three ships come sailing in,

3 And who do you think was in them then
   But Joseph and his fair lady!

4 O he did whistle and she did sing,

5 And all the bells on earth did ring,

6 And all the angels in heaven did sing

   On Christmas Day in the morning.

Traditional English

ONCE IN ROYAL DAVID'S CITY

Slow and measured

HENRY JOHN GAUNTLETT, 1805-1876, ARR. E.P.

Once in roy - al Da - vid's ci - ty Stood a
Where a mo - ther laid her ba - by In a

low - ly cat - tle shed,
man - ger for his bed: Ma - ry was that mo - ther

mild, Je - sus Christ her lit - tle child.

1 Once in royal David's city
   Stood a lowly cattle shed,
Where a mother laid her baby
   In a manger for his bed:
Mary was that mother mild,
Jesus Christ her little child.

2 He came down to earth from heaven,
   Who is God and Lord of all,
And his shelter was a stable,
   And his cradle was a stall;
With the poor, and mean, and lowly,
Lived on earth our Saviour holy.

3 And through all his wondrous childhood
   He would honour and obey,
Love and watch the lowly maiden,
   In whose gentle arms he lay:
Christian children all must be
Mild, obedient, good as he.

4 For he is our childhood's pattern:
   Day by day like us he grew,
He was little, weak, and helpless,
   Tears and smiles like us he knew;
And he feeleth for our sadness,
And he shareth in our gladness.

5 And our eyes at last shall see him,
   Through his own redeeming love,
For that child so dear and gentle
   Is our Lord in heaven above;
And he leads his children on
To the place where he is gone.

6 Not in that poor lowly stable,
   With the oxen standing by,
We shall see him; but in heaven,
   Set at God's right hand on high;
When like stars his children crowned
All in white shall wait around.

Cecil Frances Alexander, 1823-1895

O COME, ALL YE FAITHFUL

Flowing and lyrical

JOHN FRANCIS WADE, 1711-1786, ARR. E.P.

O come, all ye faith-ful, Joy-ful and tri-umph-ant, O come ye, O come ye to Beth-le-hem: Come and be-hold him, Born the King of an-gels: O come let us a-dore him, O come let us a-dore him, O come let us a-dore him, Christ the Lord.

Adeste, fideles

1 O come, all ye faithful,
Joyful and triumphant,
O come ye, O come ye to Bethlehem;
 Come and behold him,
 Born the King of angels:

  O come let us adore him,
  O come let us adore him,
  O come let us adore him, Christ the Lord.

2 God of God,
Light of Light,
Lo, he abhors not the Virgin's womb;
 Very God,
 Begotten not created:

3 Sing, choirs of angels,
Sing in exultation,
Sing, all ye citizens of heaven above;
 Glory to God
 In the highest:

4 Yea, Lord, we greet thee,
Born this happy morning,
Jesu, to thee be glory given;
 Word of the Father,
 Now in flesh appearing:

Hymn on the Prose for Christmas Day
Ascribed to John Francis Wade, 1711-1786
Translated by Frederick Oakeley, 1802-1880

DING DONG MERRILY ON HIGH

Lively   FRENCH, SIXTEENTH CENTURY, ARR. M.W.

Ding dong! mer-ri-ly on high   in heav'n the bells are ring - ing,

Ding dong! ve-ri-ly the sky   is   rent with an-gels sing - ing.

Glo -

- ri - a, Ho - san-na in ex - cel - sis.

1 Ding dong! merrily on high
      in heav'n the bells are ringing,
   Ding dong! verily the sky
      is rent with angels singing.

      Gloria, Hosanna in excelsis.

2 E'en so here below, below,
      let steeple bells be swungen,
   And io, io, io,
      by priest and people sungen.

3 Pray you, dutifully prime
      your matin chime, ye ringers;
   May you beautifully rhyme
      your evetime song, ye singers.

George Ratcliffe Woodward, 1848-1934

PATAPAN

Fast and lightly

BERNARD DE LA MONNOYE, 1641-1728, ARR. M.W.

Take thy ta-bor and thy flute, None to-day must e'er be mute: With such jol-ly shep-herd toys, Tu-re-lu-re-lu, pa-ta-pa-ta-pan; To the sound of this shrill noise, let us raise a___ No-el, Boys!

Guillo, pran ton Tamborin

1 Take thy tabor and thy flute,
   None today must e'er be mute:
   With such jolly shepherd toys,
       Tu-re-lu-re-lu, pa-ta-pa-ta-pan;
   To the sound of this shrill noise,
   Let us raise a Noel, Boys!

2 Long ago our fathers sang
   Such a song on this same day:
   'Twas of Bethlehem, their lay,
       Tu-re-lu-re-lu, pa-ta-pa-ta-pan;
   Where wise kings and shepherds stray
   To the stars their music rang.

3 As we join our choicest airs,
   In a hymn that upward fares:
   Earth and heaven seem near our prayers:
       Tu-re-lu-re-lu, pa-ta-pa-ta-pan;
   Vanish all our daily cares
   While we dance and sing Noel.

Anonymous French

CHRISTIANS, AWAKE! SALUTE
THE HAPPY MORN

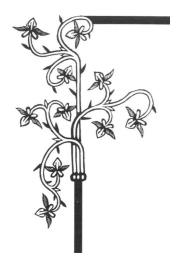

J. WAINWRIGHT, 1723-1768, ARR. M.W.

Crisp, fairly fast

Christ - ians, a - wake! Sa - lute the hap - py morn,

Where - on the Sa - viour of the world was born;

Rise to a - dore the my - ste - ry of love,

Which hosts of an - gels chan - ted from a - bove;

With them the joy - ful ti - dings first be - gun Of

God in - car - nate and the Vir - gin's Son.

CHRISTIANS, AWAKE! SALUTE
THE HAPPY MORN

1 Christians, awake! Salute the happy morn,
 Whereon the Saviour of the world was born;
 Rise to adore the mystery of love,
 Which hosts of angels chanted from above;
 With them the joyful tidings first begun
 Of God incarnate and the Virgin's Son.

2 Then to the watchful shepherds it was told,
 Who heard the angelic herald's voice, 'Behold,
 I bring good tidings of a Saviour's birth
 To you and all the nations upon earth;
 This day hath God fulfilled his promised word,
 This day is born a Saviour, Christ the Lord.'

3 He spake; and straightway the celestial choir
 In hymns of joy, unknown before, conspire.
 The praises of redeeming love they sang,
 And heaven's whole orb with Alleluyas rang:
 God's highest glory was their anthem still,
 Peace upon earth, and mutual goodwill.

4 To Bethlehem straight the enlightened shepherds ran,
 To see the wonder God had wrought for man,
 And found, with Joseph and the blessèd Maid,
 Her Son, the Saviour, in a manger laid;
 Amazed the wondrous story they proclaim,
 The first apostles of his infant fame.

5 Like Mary let us ponder in our mind
 God's wondrous love in saving lost mankind;
 Trace we the Babe, who hath retrieved our loss,
 From his poor manger to his bitter cross;
 Then may we hope, the angelic thrones among,
 To sing, redeemed, a glad triumphal song.

John Byrom, 1690-1763

WHAT CHILD IS THIS?

Soft and lyrical 'GREENSLEEVES' TRADITIONAL ENGLISH, ARR. M.W.

What child is this ___ who, laid to rest, ___ On

Ma - ry's lap ___ is sleep - ing? Whom an - gels greet ___ with

e sim.

an - thems sweet, ___ While shep - herds watch ___ are keep - ing?

This, this ___ is Christ the King, ___ Whom

shep - herds guard ___ while an - gels sing. Haste, haste ___ to

bring him praise, __ The Babe, __ the Son __ of Ma - ry!

1 What child is this who, laid to rest,
   On Mary's lap is sleeping?
   Whom angels greet with anthems sweet,
   While shepherds watch are keeping?
   This, this is Christ the King,
   Whom shepherds guard while angels sing.
   Haste, haste to bring him praise,
   The Babe, the Son of Mary!

2 Why lies he in such mean estate,
   Where ox and ass are feeding?
   Good Christians, fear: for sinners here
   The silent Word is pleading.
   Nails, spear, shall pierce him through,
   The cross be borne for me, for you.
   Hail, hail the Word made flesh,
   The Babe, the Son of Mary!

3 So bring him incense, gold and myrrh,
   Come peasant, king, to own him.
   The King of kings salvation brings,
   Let loving hearts enthrone him.
   Raise, raise the song on high,
   The Virgin sings her lullaby.
   Joy, joy for Christ is born,
   The Babe, the Son of Mary!

William Chatterton Dix, 1837-1898

GOD REST YOU MERRY,
GENTLEMEN

Cheerful, flowing

TRADITIONAL ENGLISH, ARR. E.P.

God rest you mer-ry, gen-tle-men, let no-thing you dis-

-may, For Je-sus Christ our Sa-viour Was born up-on this

day, To save us all from Sa-tan's power when we were gone a-stray:

O___ tid-ings of com-fort and joy, com-fort and

joy, O___ tid-ings of com-fort and joy.

1 God rest you merry, gentlemen,
Let nothing you dismay,
For Jesus Christ our Saviour
Was born upon this day,
To save us all from Satan's power
When we were gone astray:

O tidings of comfort and joy.

GOD REST YOU MERRY, GENTLEMEN

2 In Bethlehem in Jewry
    This blessèd babe was born,
And laid within a manger
    Upon this blessèd morn;
The which his mother Mary
    Nothing did take in scorn;

3 From God our heavenly Father
    A blessèd angel came,
And unto certain shepherds
    Brought tidings of the same,
How that in Bethlehem was born
    The Son of God by name:

4 'Fear not,' then said the angel,
    'Let nothing you afright,
This day is born a Saviour
    Of virtue, power, and might;
So frequently to vanquish all
    The friends of Satan quite':

5 The shepherds at those tidings
    Rejoicèd much in mind,
And left their flocks a-feeding
    In tempest, storm and wind,
And went to Bethlehem straightway
    This blessèd babe to find:

6 But when to Bethlehem they came,
    Whereat this infant lay,
They found him in a manger
    Where oxen feed on hay,
His mother Mary kneeling
    Unto the Lord did pray:

7 Now to the Lord sing praises,
    All you within this place,
And with true love and brotherhood
    Each other now embrace;
This holy tide of Christmas
    All others doth deface:

Traditional English

GOOD KING WENCESLAS

1 Good King Wenceslas looked out
   On the Feast of Stephen,
When the snow lay round about,
   Deep and crisp and even:
Brightly shone the moon that night,
   Though the frost was cruel,
When a poor man came in sight
   Gathering winter fuel.

2 'Hither, page, and stand by me,
   If thou know'st it, telling,
Yonder peasant, who is he?
   Where and what his dwelling?'
'Sire, he lives a good league hence,
   Underneath the mountain,
Right against the forest fence,
   By Saint Agnes' fountain.'

3 'Bring me flesh, and bring me wine,
   Bring me pine-logs hither:
Thou and I will see him dine,
   When we bear them thither.'
Page and monarch, forth they went,
   Forth they went together;
Through the rude wind's wild lament
   And the bitter weather.

4 'Sire, the night is darker now,
   And the wind blows stronger;
Fails my heart, I know not how;
   I can go no longer.'
'Mark my footsteps, good my page;
   Tread thou in them boldly:
Thou shalt find the winter's rage
   Freeze thy blood less coldly.'

5 In his master's steps he trod,
   Where the snow lay dinted;
Heat was in the very sod
   Which the Saint had printed.
Therefore, Christian men, be sure,
   Wealth or rank possessing,
Ye who now will bless the poor,
   Shall yourselves find blessing.

John Mason Neale, 1818-1866

PAST THREE A CLOCK

PAST THREE A CLOCK

Past three a clock,
And a cold frosty morning,
Past three a clock;
Good morrow, masters all!

1 Born is a Baby,
 Gentle as may be,
 Son of the eternal
 Father supernal.

Past three a clock,
And a cold frosty morning,
Past three a clock;
Good morrow, masters all!

2 Seraph quire singeth,
 Angel bell ringeth;
 Hark how they rime it,
 Time it and chime it.

3 Mid earth rejoices
 Hearing such voices
 Ne'ertofore so well
 Carolling *Nowell.*

4 Hinds o'er the pearly,
 Dewy lawn early
 Seek the high Stranger
 Laid in the manger.

5 Cheese from the dairy
 Bring they for Mary
 And, not for money,
 Butter and honey.

6 Light out of star-land
 Leadeth from far land
 Princes, to meet him,
 Worship and greet him.

7 Myrrh from full coffer,
 Incense they offer;
 Nor is the golden
 Nugget withholden.

8 Thus they: I pray you,
 Up, sirs, nor stay you
 Till ye confess him
 Likewise and bless him.

George Ratcliffe Woodward, 1848-1934

WE THREE KINGS OF ORIENT ARE

The Kings.

1 We three kings of Orient are;
  Bearing gifts we traverse afar
  Field and fountain, moor and mountain,
  Following yonder star:

  O star of wonder, star of night,
  Star with royal beauty bright,
  Westward leading, still proceeding,
  Guide us to thy perfect light.

Melchior.

2 Born a king on Bethlehem plain,
  Gold I bring, to crown him again –
  King for ever, ceasing never,
  Over us all to reign:

Gaspar.

3 Frankincense to offer have I;
  Incense owns a Deity nigh:
  Prayer and praising, all men raising,
  Worship him, God most high:

Balthazar.

4 Myrrh is mine; its bitter perfume
  Breathes a life of gathering gloom;
  Sorrowing, sighing, bleeding, dying,
  Sealed in the stone-cold tomb:

All.

5 Glorious now, behold him arise,
  King, and God, and sacrifice!
  Heaven sings alleluya,
  Alleluya the earth replies:

John Henry Hopkins, 1820-1891

BRIGHTEST AND BEST OF THE SONS OF THE MORNING

FROM *HIMMELS-LUST*, 1679, HARMONIZED BY J.S. BACH, ADAPTED BY M.W.

With quiet reverence

Brigh - test and best of the sons of the morn - ing, Dawn on our dark - ness and lend us thine aid; Star of the East, the ho - ri - zon a - dorn - ing, Guide where our in - fant Re - dee - mer is laid.

BRIGHTEST AND BEST OF THE SONS OF THE MORNING

1 Brightest and best of the sons of the morning,
    Dawn on our darkness and lend us thine aid;
Star of the East, the horizon adorning,
    Guide where our infant Redeemer is laid.

2 Cold on his cradle the dew-drops are shining,
    Low lies his head with the beasts of the stall:
Angels adore him in slumber reclining,
    Maker and Monarch and Saviour of all.

3 Say, shall we yield him, in costly devotion,
    Odours of Edom and offerings divine?
Gems of the mountain and pearls of the ocean,
    Myrrh from the forest or gold from the mine?

4 Vainly we offer each ample oblation,
    Vainly with gifts would his favour secure;
Richer by far is the heart's adoration,
    Dearer to God are the prayers of the poor.

5 Brightest and best of the sons of the morning,
    Dawn on our darkness and lend us thine aid;
Star of the East, the horizon adorning,
    Guide where our infant Redeemer is laid.

Bishop Reginald Heber, 1783-1826

rings, Four __ col - ley birds, Three French hens,

Two _ tur - tle doves and a par - tridge __ in a pear - tree.

1 On the first day of Christmas my true-love sent to me
   A partridge in a pear-tree.

2 On the second day of Christmas my true-love sent to me
   Two turtle doves
   And a partridge in a pear-tree.

3 On the third day of Christmas my true-love sent to me
   Three French hens,
   Two turtle doves
   And a partridge in a pear-tree.

4 On the fourth day of Christmas my true-love sent to me
   Four colley birds,
   Three French hens,
   Two turtle doves
   And a partridge in a pear-tree.

5 On the fifth day of Christmas my true-love sent to me
   Five gold rings,
   Four colley birds
   etc.

6   Six geese a-laying,

7   Seven swans a-swimming,

8   Eight maids a-milking,

9   Nine drummers drumming,

10 Ten pipers piping,

11 Eleven ladies dancing,

12 Twelve lords a-leaping,

Traditional English

107

SANS DAY CAROL

Like a moderately slow dance

TRADITIONAL CORNISH, ARR. M.W.

Now the hol - ly bears a ber - ry as white as the

milk, And Ma - ry bore Je - sus, all wrapp'd up in

silk: And Ma - ry bore Je - sus our Sa - viour for to

be. And the first tree in the green - wood, it

was the hol - ly. Hol - ly! Hol - ly! And the

first tree in the green - wood, it was the hol - ly!

SANS DAY CAROL

1 Now the holly bears a berry as white as the milk,
And Mary bore Jesus, all wrapped up in silk:

And Mary bore Jesus our Saviour for to be,
And the first tree in the greenwood, it was the holly.
Holly! Holly!
And the first tree in the greenwood, it was the holly!

2 Now the holly bears a berry as green as the grass,
And Mary bore Jesus, who died on the cross:

3 Now the holly bears a berry as black as the coal,
And Mary bore Jesus, who died for us all:

4 Now the holly bears a berry, as blood is it red,
Then trust we our Saviour, who rose from the dead:

Traditional English

Sans Day: Saint Day, a Breton saint venerated in Cornwall, where a
village bears his name

WASSAIL SONG

Cheerful

TRADITIONAL YORKSHIRE, ARR. E.P.

Here we come a-was-sail-ing A-mong the leaves so green, ___

Here we come a-wand-'ring, So fair ___ to be seen. Love and

joy come to you. And ___ in your was-sail too. And God

bless you and send ___ you a hap-py New

Year. And God send you a hap-py New ___ Year.

WASSAIL SONG

1 Here we come a-wassailing
    Among the leaves so green,
Here we come a-wandering
    So fair to be seen.

Love and joy come to you,
And in your wassail too,
And God bless you and send you
A happy New Year.

2 Our wassail cup is made
    Of the rosemary tree,
And so is your beer
    Of the best barley.

3 We are not daily beggars
    That beg from door to door,
But we are neighbours' children
    Whom you have seen before.

4 Good Master and good Mistress,
    As you sit by the fire,
Pray think of us poor children
    Who are wandering in the mire.

5 We have a little purse
    Made of ratching* leather skin;
We want some of your small change
    To line it well within.

6 Call up the Butler of this house,
    Put on his golden ring;
Let him bring us a glass of beer,
    And the better we shall sing.

7 Bring us out a table,
    And spread it with a cloth;
Bring us out a mouldy cheese,
    And some of your Christmas loaf.

Envoi
8 God bless the Master of this house,
    Likewise the Mistress too;
And all the little children
    That round the table go.

9 And all your kind and kinsfolk
    That dwell both far and near;
I wish you a Merry Christmas,
    And a happy New Year.

Traditional English

* *ratching*, stretching

INDEX OF TITLES
AND FIRST LINES